Winning Your Benefit Appeal
What you need to know

Child Poverty Action Group

Published by Child Poverty Action Group
30 Micawber Street
London N1 7TB
Tel: 020 7837 7979
staff@cpag.org.uk
www.cpag.org.uk
© Child Poverty Action Group 2021

This book is sold subject to the condition that it shall not, by way of trade or otherwise, be lent, resold, hired out or otherwise circulated without the publisher's prior consent in any form of binding or cover other than that in which it is published and without a similar condition including this condition being imposed on the subsequent purchaser.
A CIP record for this book is available from the British Library.
ISBN: 978 1 915324 19 1

Child Poverty Action Group is a charity registered in England and Wales (registration number 294841) and in Scotland (registration number SC039339), and is a company limited by guarantee, registered in England (registration number 1993854). VAT number: 690 808117

Cover design by Colorido Studios
Typeset by DLxml, a division of RefineCatch Limited, Bungay, Suffolk
Content management system by KonnectSoft
Printed and bound in the UK by CPI Group (UK) Ltd

Author
Simon Osborne is a welfare rights worker at CPAG.

Acknowledgements
Many thanks to Lynsey Dalton, Jessica Strode and Martin Williams for their valuable comments, Nicola Johnston for editing and managing the production, Anne Ketley for updating the index and Sarah Warburton for proofreading the text.

About Child Poverty Action Group

Child Poverty Action Group is a national charity that works on behalf of the one in four children in the UK growing up in poverty. We use our understanding of what causes poverty and the impact it has on children's lives to campaign for policies that will prevent and solve poverty – for good.

We provide trusted and expert information and advice for the welfare rights and advice community – online, and through our books, training and advice services. Our advice lines support thousands of advisers a year, helping them to give families the best information and advice. Our *Welfare Benefits Handbook*, described as the 'adviser's bible', is used by Citizens Advice bureaux, local authorities and law centres throughout the UK. We also keep advisers up to date with trends and changes in the social security system through bulletins and our highly regarded training courses and seminars.

Poverty affects one in four children in the UK today. When children grow up poor they miss out – and so do the rest of us. They miss out on the things most children take for granted: warm clothes, school trips, having friends over for tea. They do less well at school and earn less as adults. Any family can fall on hard times and find it difficult to make ends meet. But poverty is not inevitable. With the right policies every child can have the opportunity to do well in life, and we all share the rewards of having a stronger economy and a healthier, fairer society.

If you would like to join us to help end child poverty, please visit cpag.org.uk, or follow us on Facebook (facebook.com/cpaguk) and X (@cpaguk).

Keeping up to date

Advisers can get the latest information on appeals procedure and caselaw by booking on a CPAG training course. We can also provide your workplace with in-house training. See cpag.org.uk/training for more information.

Our *Welfare Benefits Handbook*, published every April, tells you all you need to know about entitlement to benefits and other payments, and contains the latest information on appeals. With up-to-date information, insights, decision-making tools and appeal letter generators, CPAG Welfare Rights is our online platform that supplements the expertise advisers have come to trust and rely on from our rights handbooks and training. CPAG Welfare Rights provides digital access to our flagship *Welfare Benefits Handbook*, which is fully searchable and updated throughout the year online. See cpag.org.uk/subscriptions to subscribe or find out more.

Getting advice

Your local Citizens Advice or other advice centre can give you advice and support on benefits. See citizensadvice.org.uk if you live in England or Wales, or cas.org.uk if you live in Scotland.

CPAG has an advice line for advisers. If you can't hear or speak on the phone, you can contact the advice line using Relay UK.

For advisers in the UK:
Telephone: 020 7812 5231, Monday to Friday 10am to 12pm and 2pm to 4pm

For advisers in Scotland:
Telephone: 0141 552 0552, Monday to Thursday 10am to 4pm and Friday 10am to 12pm
Email: advice@cpagscotland.org.uk

Contents

Chapter 1 **Introduction** 1

Chapter 2 **The appeals system** 10

Chapter 3 **Making an appeal** 25

Chapter 4 **Preparing your appeal** 56

Chapter 5 **Appeals about illness and disability** 92

Chapter 6 **Deciding your appeal** 114

Chapter 7 **After the appeal** 146

Appendix **Glossary of terms** 162

Index 168

Chapter 1
Introduction

This chapter covers:

1. What is an appeal?
2. Who is this guide for?
3. Which decisions can you appeal?
4. Representatives
5. How do you win your appeal?

What you need to know

- If you disagree with a decision about your benefit, you may be able to appeal against it.
- Appeals against benefit decisions are made to an appeal tribunal called the 'First-tier Tribunal'.
- Appeal tribunals are courts of law and must apply the law. However, they are not as formal as many courts and are not supposed to be intimidating. They are usually more concerned with establishing facts and considering evidence than with detailed disputes about the law.
- If you want to appeal, it is best to have a 'representative' if you can. You do not need to be legally qualified or a legal expert to represent yourself or someone else in an appeal.
- It is often worth appealing, as there is a high success rate. However, you may be able to avoid an appeal by providing further information or evidence.

1. What is an appeal?

If you disagree with a decision about your benefit, you can ask the 'decision maker' to look at it again.

> Box A
> **Who is the decision maker?**
>
> The decision maker is usually an officer at the DWP, HMRC (for child benefit and guardian's allowance) or local authority (for housing benefit).
>
> Some benefits have been devolved to the Scottish government – see Chapter 2 for more details. Decisions about these 'Scottish benefits' are made by an officer of Social Security Scotland.

If the decision maker looks at the decision again and you are still unhappy, you can ask an independent tribunal to reconsider the decision. This is an appeal. Usually, you must ask for a decision to be looked at again before you can appeal.

The tribunal that deals with benefit appeals is called the 'First-tier Tribunal'. It can make any decision that the decision maker could have made. This means it can 'uphold' the original decision, confirming that it is correct, or it can 'allow' the appeal and make a different decision. In some cases, the tribunal's decision may be less favourable to you than the decision maker's.

The tribunal must apply the law: it cannot make exceptions that the law does not allow. Winning your appeal means showing the tribunal how the facts and evidence in your case mean that the relevant law, when properly applied, means that you are entitled to benefit.

Tribunals can decide your appeal by holding a 'hearing' (sometimes called an 'oral hearing', conducted by telephone or video call, or in person), or without a hearing and just considering all the evidence provided in the appeal papers. Most appeals are decided at a hearing. There is more about how your appeal is decided in Chapter 6.

2. Who is this guide for?

This guide is for anyone who wants to appeal to the 'First-tier Tribunal'.

It is particularly for people with little, or no, experience. However, if you have some experience, you may also find it useful.

The information and advice in this guide is addressed to 'you' as the claimant. However, you can have a 'representative' to assist you with your appeal and to represent you at the tribunal, and this guide can also be used by them.

What does this guide cover?

This guide covers what you need to know in order to take an appeal to the First-tier Tribunal. It explains:

- the appeal process
- how to prepare for the appeal
- how to gather evidence and construct your arguments
- how to write a 'submission'
- what happens at an appeal 'hearing'

It is also possible to appeal against the First-tier Tribunal's decision. This appeal is made to a different tribunal, called the 'Upper Tribunal'. Appeals to the Upper Tribunal are more concerned with the interpretation of the law. This guide does not cover appeals to the Upper Tribunal, although there is some basic information about them in Chapter 7.

3. Which decisions can you appeal?

You can appeal about most decisions on your entitlement to social security benefits, including:

- universal credit, including whether or not you are fit for work and when your benefit is reduced because of a 'sanction'
- employment and support allowance, including whether or not you are fit for work

- personal independence payment and disability living allowance
- jobseeker's allowance
- housing benefit
- the residence tests that apply to most benefits
- 'Scottish benefits', including adult disability payment, child disability payment and Scottish child payment

There are a few decisions that you cannot appeal against – eg, decisions about how and when a benefit is paid and, if you have been overpaid universal credit, whether the 'overpayment' can be recovered from you.

Before you can appeal, you must usually have asked the 'decision maker' to look at the decision again. This is called a 'mandatory reconsideration'. There is information about this in Chapter 3.

What are most appeals about?

Many appeals are about illness or disability, and most of those concern universal credit, personal independence payment or employment and support allowance. Many of the examples in this guide are therefore about illness or disability. Although appeals about illness or disability are essentially the same as appeals about other issues, they often involve particular issues about medical evidence and the tests that decide whether or not you qualify, including whether you are fit for work. Chapter 5 covers some of the issues that arise in these appeals.

4. Representatives

You can have a 'representative' to assist you with your appeal and help you put your case to the tribunal. A representative does not need to be a lawyer or have a legal, or any other, qualification. However, the tribunal expects them to:

- know your case and the points they wish to make
- help establish the facts
- have a basic knowledge of the relevant law

What CPAG says

Having a representative

It is always better to have a representative, if you can. A representative can provide a lot of help with preparing your appeal and increase the chances of your winning it.

A good representative is likely to have access to information and resources to help with the appeal, and may have some useful experience in representing other people. They can liaise on your behalf with the various official bodies involved in your appeal, and may be able to get evidence for you and write a 'submission' to send to the tribunal.

You do not have to have a representative and you can represent yourself in your appeal if you wish, or you can get help from a friend or relative. However, having a representative involves more than just having someone with you for reassurance or emotional support (valuable though these things are). A representative must present your case to the tribunal in the most effective way. So a good representative will help prepare your appeal by gathering relevant facts and evidence, checking the law and helping you get ready for the 'hearing'.

Box B
Finding a representative

Most representatives are not lawyers or legally qualified. They are often a paid worker or volunteer working in:

- Citizens Advice bureaux
- law centres
- firms of solicitors doing social security work
- local authority welfare rights units
- local disability charities or support groups
- unemployed workers' centres or trade unions
- hospitals and social services departments

If you do not have a representative, the tribunal does not expect you to do their job. Instead, it asks you about the basic facts in your case, such as your medical condition and what happened at your medical assessment. There is more information about the role of representatives in Chapter 4.

5. How do you win your appeal?

What CPAG says

Winning your appeal

To increase your chance of success, do the following.

- Ask for a 'hearing' of your appeal, so that the tribunal can ask you questions, clarify facts and discuss the evidence.

- Have a 'representative', if possible. They can help check the law, gather evidence, write a 'submission', and assist you and the tribunal at the hearing.

- Be well prepared. Understand what the tribunal is like and what it can do. Be ready to answer any questions it may have.

Is it worth appealing?

It is often worth appealing. Success rates are high, although they vary depending on the benefit concerned, whether there is a hearing of the appeal (rather than just on the basis of the appeal papers) and whether you are represented. Many decisions are matters of judgement or opinion, and another view of the same facts and evidence could be made. Sometimes, things simply go wrong.

However, there is no point appealing against a decision that is clearly legally correct, as this cannot be changed by the tribunal. For example, you may be disappointed by the amount of benefit you are paid, but if your award has been calculated correctly, the tribunal is bound by the law that sets the rates and cannot change the decision.

Box C
Decisions worth appealing: examples

- A decision about the 'work capability assessment' that determines whether you are fit for work, or can be expected to look for work, for universal credit or employment and support allowance. The official medical report may be inaccurate, or the 'decision maker' may have ignored evidence or not obtained evidence from someone who knows you.

- A decision about the disability tests for personal independence payment, disability living allowance and attendance allowance (or Scottish disability benefits such as adult disability payment). The official medical report may be inaccurate, or the decision maker may have ignored evidence or not obtained evidence from someone who knows you.

- A decision involving the decision maker's judgement, such as whether you are living with another person as a couple, whether you deliberately got rid of money in order to get benefit, or whether you have a 'right to reside' in the UK.

- A decision involving a complex legal issue which the decision maker may have misunderstood or wrongly applied.

What CPAG says

Successful appeals

The overall success rate for appeals dealt with at a hearing is high – over 60 per cent – although it varies between individual benefits. Success rates are generally much lower if the appeal is decided without a hearing – ie, just on the basis of the appeal papers.

If a representative has helped with the appeal, rates can be higher still. Many representatives report success rates at hearings of well over 70 per cent.

1 / Introduction

Can an appeal be avoided?

An appeal is often necessary to correct an inaccurate or poor decision. However, as appeals are time consuming for everyone involved and can be stressful, you should consider whether an appeal can be avoided.

> Box D
> **Avoiding an appeal**
>
> - Is the decision wrong, or can you at least argue that it is wrong? For example, is it based on a judgement that could be challenged? Is it based on facts that have been misunderstood? If the decision is clearly correct, the tribunal cannot change it.
> - Is there an obvious simple mistake in the decision that can be pointed out to the decision maker, which clearly means the decision should be changed without the need for an appeal?
> - Is there any further information or evidence that might persuade the decision maker to change their decision without the need for an appeal?
> - If you must ask for the decision to be looked at again before you can appeal, is there further information or evidence that you could send with this request, so that the decision is changed without the need for an appeal?

The most effective way of avoiding an appeal is to make the decision maker aware of information or evidence they did not use when making their original decision. For example, you could correct something that was misunderstood in a medical examination, provide supportive medical evidence from your GP or some other source, or provide evidence that your income is different from that used by the decision maker. Decision makers are trained to be prepared to consider such information or evidence, even after they have made their decision, and to change their initial decision if appropriate.

If you must ask for the decision to be looked at again before you can appeal (a 'mandatory reconsideration'), this provides an opportunity to send further information or evidence.

Note: you can still provide further information or evidence after the appeal has been made.

Chapter 2
The appeals system

This chapter covers:

1. Who deals with your appeal?
2. Who is on the tribunal?
3. Where does the appeal hearing take place?
4. What decisions can the tribunal make?
5. How long does the appeal process take?
6. Who deals with appeals about Scottish benefits?

What you need to know

- Tribunals are independent courts of law, but are not as formal as many courts.
- There is always a judge with legal expertise on the tribunal panel and there may be up to two other members. A 'tribunal clerk' administers the appeal.
- The tribunal 'hearing' may take place in person at a venue in a nearby town or city, or by telephone or video call.
- The tribunal reconsiders the decision being appealed. It can confirm or change it, and can even make a less favourable decision.
- Tribunals cannot award costs or compensation.
- Large numbers of appeals are received and dealt with every year, and the process is likely to take several months.

1. Who deals with your appeal?

Most appeals are administered by 'HM Courts and Tribunals Service'. The tribunal itself is called the 'First-tier Tribunal'. It is independent and has between one and three members. A clerk assists with the administration.

Appeals about the 'Scottish benefits' paid by Social Security Scotland are administered by the 'Scottish Courts and Tribunals Service', but are still called First-tier Tribunals. See section 6 of this chapter for more information.

HM Courts and Tribunals Service

The appeals system for most appeals is administered by HM Courts and Tribunals Service. This is an agency of the Ministry of Justice. Although it is a government body, it is independent of the organisations that make the initial decisions on your benefits, such as the DWP. The people who sit on the tribunals are completely independent of all government departments.

The First-tier Tribunal

The First-tier Tribunal considers appeals against decisions by:

- the DWP about benefits such as universal credit, employment and support allowance and personal independence payment
- HMRC about child benefit and guardian's allowance
- local authorities about housing benefit

For administrative purposes, the First-tier Tribunal is organised into a number of different 'chambers' to hear different sorts of appeals. The chambers have different membership and sometimes slightly different rules. Benefit appeals are always included in the 'Social Entitlement Chamber' of the First-tier Tribunal. So if you come across a reference to the Social Entitlement Chamber, this refers to the type of tribunal that considers benefit appeals.

What does the tribunal clerk do?

Tribunal clerks deal with the administration of appeals. They send out the papers relating to the appeal, set the date for the 'hearing' and assist the tribunal with the administration on the day of the hearing. Clerks can also make some decisions in the run-up to the hearing – eg, about whether your appeal has been properly made. In practice, you deal with the clerk quite a lot before the hearing, so it is important to have a good working relationship with them.

2. Who is on the tribunal?

What the law says

Members of the tribunal

The tribunal is made up of one, two or three members, depending on the type of appeal. There is always at least a member with legal expertise, called the 'judge'.

Depending on the type of appeal, there may also be a medically qualified member and a disability qualified member.

Practice Statement of the Senior President of Tribunals, 'Composition of Tribunals in Social Security and Child Support Cases in the Social Entitlement Chamber on or after 1 August 2013'; The First-tier Tribunal for Scotland Social Security Chamber and Upper Tribunal for Scotland (Composition) Regulations 2018

The judge

The judge of the tribunal must have legal expertise. Often this means that judges are solicitors or barristers with at least five years' experience, although not all judges have a legal qualification. The judge knows about the law relevant to your appeal, but is not required to have worked in social security – eg, they may have worked as a solicitor in family or criminal law. For appeals about 'Scottish benefits', they are called the 'legal member'.

The judge chairs the hearing and provides the tribunal with legal expertise.

The medically qualified member

The medically qualified member provides the medical expertise for the tribunal. They must be a registered medical practitioner. Usually, the medical member is a doctor, such as a GP, but need not have specialist knowledge in the area relevant to your appeal. They are not required to have a legal qualification. They may also carry out medical examinations for the DWP medical service, but will not have previously been involved in the decision you are appealing.

The disability qualified member

The disability qualified member provides expertise about the effects of disability. They must be experienced in dealing with disability, through having a disability themselves, being a carer or working with people with disabilities – eg, as a physiotherapist, occupational therapist or social worker. The disability qualified member cannot be a doctor. They are not required to have a legal qualification.

The composition of the tribunal

The rules on the composition of the tribunal are fixed in law, and you cannot ask for a differently comprised tribunal. There are some exceptions.

- If your case is about a legal question and the medical and disability members are not necessary, a judge may hear the appeal alone.
- There can be a second doctor if your appeal involves complex medical issues, particularly in an industrial injuries disablement benefit case.
- If your case involves examining financial accounts, an accountant may sit with the judge to hear the appeal.

- If your appeal involves complex medical issues, but is not about a benefit that requires a two- or three-person panel, the tribunal could also include a doctor.
- A hearing can go ahead without one or more of the members usually required, but there must always be a judge present.

What the law says

Tribunal composition

- **A three-person tribunal**, comprising a judge, a medically qualified member and a disability qualified member, hears appeals about disability living allowance, personal independence payment and attendance allowance. (In the future, the law may be changed slightly so that this will only apply if the appeal is about the disability assessment for these benefits. A similar rule already applies to appeals about Scottish disability benefits such as adult disability payment.)

- **A two-person tribunal**, comprising a judge and a medically qualified member, hears appeals about the 'work capability assessment' for employment and support allowance and universal credit, and about industrial injuries disablement benefit (unless it is about a declaration of an industrial accident).

- **A judge sitting alone** hears all other appeals.

Practice Statement of the Senior President of Tribunals, 'Composition of Tribunals in Social Security and Child Support Cases in the Social Entitlement Chamber on or after 1 August 2013'; The First-tier Tribunal for Scotland Social Security Chamber and Upper Tribunal for Scotland (Composition) Regulations 2018

Have you got more than one appeal?

What the law says

Appeals about more than one benefit

Limited capability for work and personal independence payment/disability living allowance appeals should be heard in 'completely separate sessions by completely differently composed tribunals'.

Upper Tribunal decision, MB and Others v Secretary of State for Work and Pensions (ESA and DLA) [2013] UKUT 111 (AAC)

You may have appealed against decisions about different benefits, and so may have more than one appeal underway at the same time.

In general, your appeals are considered separately, but they can be considered during the same tribunal session – ie, on the same day. However, if your appeals are about personal independence payment and employment and support allowance, they must be heard by completely different tribunals in different sessions.

EXAMPLE

Tribunals hearing more than one appeal

Alessia has appealed against a decision refusing her personal independence payment. She has also appealed against a decision imposing a sanction on her universal credit for leaving her job without good reason.

Alessia's two appeals are heard by the 'First-tier Tribunal'. The tribunals that consider them must be different: a three-person tribunal for the personal independence payment appeal and a judge sitting alone for her universal credit appeal. In practice, both appeals could be considered during the same tribunal session, but they are heard separately.

> **EXAMPLE**
>
> **Tribunals hearing more than one appeal**
>
> Kyle has appealed against a decision refusing him personal independence payment. He has also appealed against a decision about his universal credit that he is fit for work because he fails the work capability assessment.
>
> Kyle's two appeals are heard by the First-tier Tribunal. Even though the issues in them overlap because they both concern how Kyle's illness affects him, the tribunals that consider them must be different: a three-person tribunal for the personal independence payment appeal and a two-person tribunal for the universal credit appeal. The appeals must be completely separate – they must be considered in different sessions and by tribunals comprising different people.

3. Where does the appeal hearing take place?

Most appeals are decided at a 'hearing'. This is an oral hearing, which you take part in. The tribunal considers your appeal having looked at the appeal papers, asked you some questions, and given you a chance to explain why you are unhappy with the decision. A hearing may be conducted by telephone or video call, which you usually take part in from home. Alternatively, the hearing may be held in person at a tribunal venue.

There is no specific rule about where an in-person appeal hearing must take place. There are tribunal venues in a number of towns and cities. Some are purpose built, but many are in places like county court or magistrates' court buildings, or civic centres. The venue should be accessible for people with disabilities. If your hearing is going to take place in person and you have any particular needs at the venue (eg, for a hearing loop or because of mobility problems, or an interpreter), tell the clerk in advance. The clerk will make sure that you can access and use the venue. If you have particular needs about a hearing conducted by telephone or video link, again tell the clerk in advance.

If you have chosen not to have a hearing at all, the tribunal will instead consider your appeal 'on the papers' – ie, without a hearing and without you taking part or being asked questions.

At the tribunal venue for an in-person hearing, there is usually a waiting room and a separate room where the appeal hearing takes place. If you are anxious in the waiting room, you can ask whether there is a private room available, although these are not available at all venues.

Chapter 6 has more information about the appeal hearing.

Can you attend the hearing?

When you appeal, you are asked if you want your appeal to be decided at a hearing.

You can ask for the hearing to be by telephone, video call or in person. However, it is up to the tribunal which of these should apply. You attend telephone or video hearings from your home. In-person hearings take place at a tribunal venue.

What CPAG says

Attending the hearing

It is best to have a hearing of your appeal and to attend the hearing so that the tribunal can speak to you. If you have a 'representative', they can attend the hearing with you and can help you. This applies whether the hearing is conducted by telephone or video (in which case you can attend from home) or in person.

An in-person hearing usually provides the very best opportunity for the tribunal to see you as well as speak to you, but this does require you to go to a tribunal venue. If you think a telephone or video hearing is not appropriate for you and want to have an in-person hearing, explain that to the tribunal when you make your appeal or when the tribunal contacts you about your appeal.

If an in-person hearing is arranged and the tribunal venue is too far for you to attend, it may be possible to have it rescheduled to one that is nearer. In that case, you should be given another opportunity to say that you would like to attend the hearing. In very exceptional cases, if you are unable to attend the tribunal venue at any time, the hearing can take place somewhere else, such as in your home. This type of hearing is called a 'domiciliary hearing'. You can request a domiciliary hearing and your request must be properly considered. In practice, however, such hearings are now rare.

What the law says

Rescheduled hearings

A tribunal should not assume that a claimant who does not want a hearing because the venue is too far from their home would also not attend a hearing rescheduled at a venue that is closer.

Upper Tribunal decision, TA v Secretary of State for Work and Pensions (PIP) [2018] UKUT 26 (AAC)

There is more about the different ways of holding a hearing in Chapter 6.

4. What decisions can the tribunal make?

The tribunal can either confirm or change the decision being appealed.

If the tribunal confirms the decision, it is not changed. This is called 'upholding' the decision.

If the tribunal changes the decision to give you what you have asked for, this is sometimes called 'allowing' your appeal.

> **EXAMPLE**
>
> **Allowing an appeal**
>
> Chloe appeals against the decision that she has failed the 'work capability assessment' and so does not have 'limited capability for work' for her universal credit claim. The tribunal considers that she has scored sufficient points to pass the assessment and so changes the decision. It allows her appeal.

Changing the decision means that the tribunal substitutes the decision being appealed with one it considers to be correct. However, it does not have to make exactly the decision you have asked for.

For example, it may change the decision about your entitlement to personal independence payment to give you the 'daily living component' at the rate you asked for, but not award you the 'mobility component'. This is sometimes called allowing your appeal 'in part'.

The tribunal can make or remake whatever decision could have been made by the 'decision maker'. Sometimes, this is described as 'standing in the decision maker's shoes': the tribunal is reconsidering the decision that is being appealed – nothing more and nothing less.

> **EXAMPLE**
>
> **Allowing an appeal in part**
>
> Esme appeals against the decision not to award her personal independence payment. The tribunal decides to change the decision being appealed to make an award of personal independence payment. However, the tribunal makes the award at a lower rate than Esme asked for. It allows her appeal in part.

> **EXAMPLE**
>
> **Allowing an appeal in part**
>
> John appeals against the decision that he failed the work capability assessment and so is not entitled to employment and support allowance. He argues, firstly, that he passes the work capability assessment and so is entitled to employment and support allowance and, secondly, that he should be awarded the support component.
>
> The tribunal allows John's appeal in part. It decides that he satisfies the work capability assessment (and so is entitled to employment and support allowance), but it does not agree that he meets the conditions for the support component.

Can the tribunal make a less favourable decision?

Because it can make whatever decision could have been made by the decision maker, a tribunal has the power to change a decision but make another that is less favourable to you than the one you appealed against.

For example, you may have appealed against being refused the daily living component of personal independence payment, but you do not want the tribunal to change your award of the mobility component, because you are happy with this. However, because you are appealing against the decision about your overall entitlement to personal independence payment, and the decision maker could allow or refuse either or both components, the tribunal could 'uphold' the part of the decision about the care component and also remove the award of the mobility component.

This is uncommon but can happen, particularly in appeals about illness and disability issues. Chapter 5 has more information about these appeals.

Can the tribunal award compensation or costs?

The tribunal cannot change the law: it must apply the law as it stands. Because it is applying social security law, it has no power to look at complaints about administration.

The tribunal cannot award costs or damages to anyone involved in the appeal. So, for example, it cannot order that you be paid compensation, or that your and your 'representative's' costs be paid, or that you must pay someone else's costs.

> **EXAMPLE**
>
> **What the tribunal can and cannot do**
>
> Ivan was refused the element for 'limited capability for work-related activity' in his universal credit, because he was not considered to satisfy the test for that in the work capability assessment. He considered that his problems with social engagement and coping with change meant that he should have passed this test and so appealed against this decision. At the hearing, Ivan tells the tribunal that he is unhappy about the medical examination he attended and felt the doctor asked him rude and unhelpful questions. He asks that he be paid compensation for his upset and inconvenience.
>
> The tribunal allows Ivan's appeal, because it considers that he passes the test for limited capability for work-related activity in the work capability assessment. So he is entitled to the limited capability for work-related activity element. However, the tribunal cannot award him any compensation for his bad experience at the medical examination – this was not part of the decision being appealed.

5. How long does the appeal process take?

'HM Courts and Tribunals Service' deals with a large number of appeals every year. It may take some time for your appeal to be decided. The amount of time it takes from receiving an appeal at HM Courts and Tribunals Service to notifying you of the outcome is known as the 'clearance time'.

Clearance times can vary from year to year but in general take months rather than weeks. However, the time may also vary between different benefits: tribunals comprising a judge sitting alone (eg, some universal credit appeals) can take less time to clear than average; tribunals with other members (eg, a personal independence payment appeal) can take more time to clear than average.

Clearance times also vary between different parts of the country. Your 'representative' may know how long the appeal process takes in your area and may be able to advise you how long you are likely to have to wait.

What CPAG says

Waiting for your appeal

You can expect to wait at least several weeks, possibly several months, for your appeal to be decided.

This waiting time can be very difficult, as you are likely to be in financial need, and your circumstances may change while you are waiting for your appeal – eg, your health may worsen or improve. Get advice about which benefits you might be able to get while you are waiting for your appeal to be dealt with.

You can ask the tribunal clerk to try to ensure that your appeal is heard as early as possible – sometimes this is called 'expediting' your appeal. Try to provide particular reasons why your appeal needs to be heard quickly – eg, if your health is at risk or if you may be evicted from your home.

6. Who deals with appeals about Scottish benefits?

In Scotland, some benefit appeals (eg, those about universal credit) are administered by 'HM Courts and Tribunals Service', as they are elsewhere in Great Britain. However, responsibility for certain benefits has been devolved to the Scottish government and new benefits are being introduced. Appeals about these 'Scottish benefits' are administered by the 'Scottish Courts and Tribunals Service'. So, for example, the Scottish Courts and Tribunals Service deals with appeals about adult disability payment.

The tribunal that deals with the appeals is called (as for other benefit appeals) the 'First-tier Tribunal'. Like tribunals for other benefit appeals, this tribunal is independent, has between one and three members, and has a clerk to assist with administration.

What are the Scottish benefits?

Responsibility for certain benefits has been devolved to the Scottish government. In this book, we call them the 'Scottish benefits'. This does *not* include a number of benefits, including universal credit, housing benefit, employment and support allowance, child benefit and retirement pensions. These benefits continue to be paid in Scotland by the UK government.

> Box A
> **Scottish benefits available in 2024**
> - adult disability payment (a separate pension-age disability payment is due to begin being introduced in 2024)
> - carer support payment, carer's allowance supplement and young carer grant
> - Best Start grants
> - child disability payment
> - child winter heating payment
> - funeral support payment
> - Scottish child payment
> - winter heating payment (a separate pension-age winter heating payment is due to be introduced in winter 2024)

Decisions about Scottish benefits are made by Social Security Scotland, and appeals about them are administered by the Scottish Courts and Tribunals Service.

The Scottish Courts and Tribunals Service

The Scottish Courts and Tribunals Service is an independent body. It is independent of the organisation that makes the initial decisions (for Scottish benefits, this is Social Security Scotland), and the people that sit on the tribunals are completely independent of all government departments.

For administrative purposes, the tribunal that deals with appeals about the Scottish benefits is part of the 'Social Security Chamber of the First-tier Tribunal for Scotland'. So if you are appealing about a Scottish benefit, you may see reference to the Scottish Courts and Tribunals Service, and also to the Social Security Chamber.

Further information

The Scottish Courts and Tribunals Service has information about the Social Security Chamber at socialsecuritychamber.scot.

Chapter 3
Making an appeal

This chapter covers:

1. Can you appeal?
2. Which decisions can be appealed?
3. What is a mandatory reconsideration?
4. Is there a time limit for appealing?
5. How do you make a valid appeal?
6. How do you make an appeal about a Scottish benefit?

What you need to know

- You can appeal against most benefit decisions.
- Usually, before you can appeal you must ask for the decision to be looked at again and have your request considered. This is usually called a 'mandatory reconsideration'. This does not apply to housing benefit or to some decisions about employment and support allowance.
- Usually, you must appeal within one month of the date of the decision, although in some circumstances this can be extended.
- Your appeal must be made in writing and contain certain information, including your reasons ('grounds') for the appeal.
- Appeals following a mandatory reconsideration are made directly to 'HM Courts and Tribunals Service'. Housing benefit appeals are made to the local authority that made the decision.
- Appeals against decisions about 'Scottish benefits' are similar, but there are some differences.

3 / Making an appeal

1. Can you appeal?

Before you can appeal against a benefit decision, the following must apply.

- You must have been sent a 'decision notice'.
- The decision must have the right of appeal – ie, it must be one that you can appeal.
- Usually, the 'decision maker' must have looked at the decision again. This is called a 'mandatory reconsideration'. They must have made a decision about this and sent it to you in a 'mandatory reconsideration notice'.

> Box A
> **Scottish benefits**
>
> If you have claimed one of the 'Scottish benefits', the decision on your claim is called a 'determination'. Before you can appeal, the decision maker must have looked at the decision again in a 'redetermination'. Rules and procedures about making an appeal about Scottish benefits are described in section 6 of this chapter.

Have you been sent a decision notice?

Once you have made a valid claim for a benefit, your claim is referred to a decision maker. The decision maker decides whether or not you are entitled and how much you can get.

If the decision is one you can appeal, you must be sent a written notice informing you of the decision and of your right to appeal. You can appeal against most decisions.

Unless it is a housing benefit decision, this decision notice also tells you that you must ask for the decision to be looked at again before you can appeal.

Decision notices about universal credit may be sent to your online journal, rather than through the post.

Decisions about employment and support allowance, universal credit if you are claiming on the basis of being too ill for work or personal independence payment usually include details of the number of points you have been awarded in your medical assessment. Decisions about universal credit usually contain details of how your entitlement has been calculated, including what income or capital has been taken into account.

If you are already getting a benefit and your circumstances change (eg, your income increases or decreases, or your health improves or deteriorates), this can mean a new decision on your entitlement is made. You are sent a decision notice telling you about the change in your entitlement and informing you of your right to appeal and (except for housing benefit) that you must ask for the decision to be looked at again before you can appeal.

Decision notices can vary, but they are always:

- in writing
- from a decision maker
- about your benefit entitlement

Who else can appeal?

You can appeal, as the claimant of the benefit. In addition, the following people can appeal against a decision about all benefits, except housing benefit:

- someone authorised to act on your behalf (known as an 'appointee')
- someone claiming personal independence payment, disability living allowance or attendance allowance on your behalf if you are terminally ill (even if this is without your knowledge)
- someone from whom an 'overpayment' of benefit can be recovered
- your partner, if the decision concerns whether they failed to take part in a 'work-focused interview' without having a good cause
- someone appointed by the DWP or HMRC to proceed with a claim for benefit for someone who has died

The following people can appeal against a decision about housing benefit:

- someone acting for you because you cannot act yourself – eg, an appointee
- someone from whom an overpayment can be recovered – eg, your landlord
- a landlord or agent if it has been decided to make (or not to make) payments of housing benefit directly to you

2. Which decisions can be appealed?

Most decisions about benefits, including all decisions about your entitlement, can be appealed. When you can appeal against a decision, it is sometimes said to 'carry the right of appeal'.

Some decisions cannot be appealed. These are usually about the way your benefit is paid, such as when or how payments are made. A few specific decisions, such as about entitlement to an advance of benefit or a budgeting advance of universal credit, cannot be appealed.

The 'decision notice' informing you of your entitlement states whether you have a right to appeal. If you think you can appeal, but the 'decision maker' does not, ask for your appeal to be forwarded to 'HM Courts and Tribunals Service'. You should state clearly why you believe you have a right to appeal against the decision in question.

Remember that a decision saying that you have been overpaid is a decision about your entitlement. Usually, the decision is about a specific issue. For example, the decision could be saying that you have been overpaid because of the calculation of your income for universal credit or the points you have been awarded in the assessment for personal independence payment for a particular activity. All these sorts of things can be part of the 'overpayment' decision and so carry the right of appeal.

Appeal rights

Decision	Can you appeal?
You have been awarded universal credit following 'managed migration' from legacy benefits/tax credits	Yes
Your universal credit has been reduced after a 'sanction'	Yes
Your employment and support allowance is stopped because you fail the 'work capability assessment'	Yes
You are not awarded the 'limited capability for work-related activity' element in your universal credit	Yes
Your care and mobility needs are not regarded as sufficient to get personal independence payment	Yes
You cannot be paid by cheque	No
You cannot be paid a budgeting advance	No
You do not satisfy the 'right to reside' test	Yes
Your housing benefit is reduced because of the 'bedroom tax'	Yes
Your benefit is reduced because you failed without good reason to take part in a 'work-focused interview'	Yes
Your income is too high for universal credit	Yes
You have been overpaid benefit	Yes
An overpayment of universal credit will be recovered from you	No
Your universal credit has been stopped because the DWP says that you have failed to confirm your identity	Yes
The DWP has refused your request that your universal credit be backdated	Yes

Can decisions about overpayments be appealed?

If you have been paid more benefit than you are entitled to, this is called an overpayment. This could be, for example, because it has been decided that your entitlement has been calculated incorrectly or because it has been decided that you did not meet, or stopped meeting, one of the basic conditions for entitlement.

What the law says

Appeals about overpayments

A decision that you have been overpaid can be appealed, because it is a decision about your entitlement.

In some cases, a decision about whether an overpayment of benefit can be recovered from you can also be appealed. However, a decision about recovering overpayments of universal credit (or 'new-style' employment and support allowance and jobseeker's allowance paid under the universal credit system) cannot be appealed. Instead, you must dispute this with the decision maker at the DWP.

Sections 71 and 71ZB Social Security Administration Act 1992

You should be sent a decision changing your entitlement to the correct amount, telling you about the overpayment and saying whether or not you must pay it back – ie, whether it is recoverable from you.

You can appeal about whether or not you have been overpaid. However, you do not always have the right to appeal about whether the overpayment can be recovered from you.

EXAMPLE

Appealing against an overpayment decision

Jordon has received a decision saying that he was not entitled to the universal credit he was paid during July and August, that he has therefore been overpaid and that he must repay the money.

Jordon can appeal against the decision that he was not entitled to universal credit during July and August. He must ask for the decision to be looked at again (a 'mandatory reconsideration') first. However, he cannot appeal against the decision that he must repay the money he was paid during this time if the decision about his entitlement is found to be correct.

If Jordon accepts that he was not entitled to universal credit, although he cannot appeal about the recovery of the overpayment, he can dispute it with the DWP. For example, he could argue that recovering the overpayment from him will cause him severe hardship.

3. What is a mandatory reconsideration?

What the law says

Mandatory reconsideration

There is a right of appeal only after a decision maker has 'considered on an application whether to revise the decision' (ie, there has been a mandatory reconsideration) if the written decision included a statement specifically saying that.

Regulation 7 The Universal Credit, Personal Independence Payment, Jobseeker's Allowance and Employment and Support Allowance (Decisions and Appeals) Regulations 2013; regulation 3ZA The Social Security and Child Support (Decisions and Appeals) Regulations 1999

Usually, before you can appeal you must ask for the decision you are unhappy with to be looked at again. You must do so within a certain period of time and your request must be considered by a 'decision maker'. This is known as a 'mandatory reconsideration'.

Note: when you ask for a mandatory reconsideration of a decision, the decision maker is able to look at the whole of the decision again. This means that they can go on to make a new decision which could be different from the one you have asked to be looked at again. The new decision could be less favourable to you than the one it replaces. Although that is not a common outcome, it happens in some cases.

You do not need to have had a mandatory reconsideration before you can appeal against a decision about housing benefit.

If the decision is that you are not entitled to employment and support allowance because you have failed the 'work capability assessment', you may not need to have had a mandatory reconsideration before you can appeal. This applies if it is the first time a decision has been made about whether you pass the work capability assessment, or if you have had other decisions about this and the previous decisions were that you had passed the assessment. In these situations, you can appeal straight away and you can still be paid some employment and support allowance while you are waiting for your appeal to be heard. The DWP should tell you if this applies to you – ask if you are unsure.

What the law says

Employment and support allowance decisions

If someone has been refused employment and support allowance due to failing the work capability assessment, but would be able to get employment and support allowance while waiting for the appeal to be heard, there is no requirement for a mandatory reconsideration before there is a right of appeal.

High Court case, R (Connor) v Secretary of State for Work and Pensions [2020] EWHC 1999 (Admin)

The basic time limit for requesting a mandatory reconsideration is within one month of the date you are sent the decision, but there is an absolute time limit of 13 months. You have a right of appeal if you apply within either of these time limits. You can still ask for a mandatory reconsideration after 13 months, but then you only have the right of appeal against a refusal to look at the decision again in cases of 'official error'.

What the law says

Time limits for mandatory reconsideration

There is a right of appeal against a benefit decision where the mandatory reconsideration was requested after one month but within the absolute time limit of 13 months, even if the decision maker has refused to look at the decision again, and irrespective of why the request was late.

Upper Tribunal reported decision, *R (CJ) and SG v Secretary of State for Work and Pensions (ESA)* [2017] UKUT 324 (AAC), reported as [2018] AACR 5

When the decision maker looks at a decision again as part of a mandatory reconsideration, they carry out a 'revision'.

You are sent a decision about the outcome of the mandatory reconsideration in a letter, usually called a 'mandatory reconsideration notice'. This tells you whether the decision you are unhappy about has been changed or not. It also tells you about your right to appeal. The letter may not always have the words 'mandatory reconsideration notice' at the top, but the phrase usually appears in it. At this point, if you are still unhappy, you can appeal.

The mandatory reconsideration process does not apply to housing benefit. You can ask for a decision on your housing benefit to be looked at again if you wish before you appeal, but you do not have to.

Box B
The mandatory reconsideration process

- Step 1: receive a 'decision notice' from the decision maker
- Step 2: apply to the decision maker for the decision to be reconsidered
- Step 3: receive a mandatory reconsideration notice
- Step 4: send your appeal to 'HM Courts and Tribunals Service'

What CPAG says

Mandatory reconsideration

If you ask for a mandatory reconsideration within a month, the decision maker must look at the decision again and you have a right of appeal. If you miss that basic time limit but make your request within the absolute 13-month time limit, the decision maker may refuse to look at the decision again, but you still have the right of appeal, whatever the reason that your request was late. So it is always advisable to make your request within a month where possible, but in any case you should do so within 13 months. After that, you will have to rely on there being an official error in the original decision in order to have a right of appeal.

What CPAG says

Housing benefit decisions

Asking for a housing benefit decision to be looked at again is one way of avoiding an appeal. The way in which you do this is the same as the way in which you apply for a mandatory reconsideration of a benefit decision. However, unless the local authority has made a very simple and obvious mistake in its decision, it may be better to appeal straight away. If you appeal, the local authority should look at the decision again anyway.

Note: if you are already getting benefit and your circumstances change (eg, your income increases), the decision awarding you benefit may be looked at again. This is called a 'supersession'. It is not a mandatory reconsideration. If you are unhappy with the new decision you get following a change in your circumstances, before you can appeal you must ask for this to be looked at again in a mandatory reconsideration.

How do you apply for a mandatory reconsideration?

You can request a mandatory reconsideration of a benefit decision in writing or verbally – eg, over the telephone. It is better to request it in writing, as you can keep a copy in case there is a dispute about whether, or when, you made the request. For universal credit, it is best to make the request on your online journal.

The DWP has a form for requesting a mandatory reconsideration which you can download, complete and send in. You do not have to use the form. The form is available at gov.uk/government/publications/challenge-a-decision-made-by-the-department-for-work-and-pensions-dwp.

When you make your request, you do not have to use the words 'mandatory reconsideration' or 'revision'. The key point is that you ask for the decision to be looked at again. However, in practice, it is clearer if you ask specifically for a 'mandatory reconsideration'.

It is best if your request is received by the decision maker within the basic time limit of one month of the date the decision was sent to you.

What the law says

Month

A month is a calendar month. For example, one calendar month from 1 June is 1 July.

Schedule 1 Interpretation Act 1978

If your request is made within this time limit, a mandatory reconsideration must then be carried out. See below for what to do if you miss the basic time limit.

This basic time limit can be extended by 14 days if the decision did not contain a written 'statement of reasons' and you request one within the month. In practice, however, this rarely happens as most decisions are regarded as already including such a statement.

> **EXAMPLE**
>
> **Applying for a mandatory reconsideration**
>
> Cole has received a decision, dated 1 June, saying that he is not entitled to an extra element in his universal credit because, following a 'work capability assessment', he is considered not to have 'limited capability for work-related activity'.
>
> Cole thinks he should be assessed as having limited capability for work-related activity and so should get the element for that in his universal credit. On 25 June, he phones the DWP and requests that the decision be looked at again. He also makes the request on his online journal, to ensure there is a written record of his request. He does not need to prove anything more for a mandatory reconsideration to take place.
>
> A decision maker looks at the decision again and carries out a revision. The decision maker concludes that the original decision is correct and should not be changed. Cole is sent the decision in a mandatory reconsideration notice. He can now appeal against the decision to the 'First-tier Tribunal'.

If you request a mandatory reconsideration within the time limit, you do not need to give any reasons (or 'grounds') for why the decision should be changed. The decision you request is therefore sometimes called called a revision on 'any grounds'.

Have you missed the basic time limit?

If you have missed the basic one-month time limit, a late mandatory reconsideration of a benefit decision can still be carried out for any reason (on any grounds) if you apply within the absolute time limit of 13 months. You still have a right of appeal, even if the decision maker refuses to look at the decision again. Make it clear that you are making a late request for a mandatory reconsideration. The decision maker can carry out a revision of the decision for any reason (on any grounds) if you make your request within:

- 13 months of the date you were notified of the decision
- 13 months of the date the one-month time limit expired if the decision is about universal credit or personal independence payment

Make sure you enable the decision to be identified in your application and include a summary of the reasons why it is late.

For a revision to be carried out on any grounds, the decision maker must be satisfied that it is reasonable to do so and that there are 'special circumstances' why you did not apply in time. Special circumstances are not defined.

> **EXAMPLE**
>
> **Applying for a late mandatory reconsideration**
>
> On 5 March, Mary was sent a decision about her personal independence payment. This told her that she was not entitled to the 'mobility component' as she could walk and did not need anyone with her when she was outdoors.
>
> Mary experiences extreme anxiety and depression, and the decision came at a bad time for her. She was too unwell to do anything about it until 10 June, when she went to her local advice centre for help.
>
> The advice centre helped her to make a late request for a mandatory reconsideration, explaining that it was late because Mary had been in a period of particular bad health after receiving the decision and had not been able to deal with any

correspondence. It enclosed a letter from her GP confirming this. The adviser also pointed out in the request that Mary's health problems have always meant that she needs a companion when she goes out – something that has been accepted in the past, and her health has not got any better.

The decision maker accepts Mary's late request and looks at the decision again. The decision maker confirms the original decision and so Mary still does not get the mobility component. Mary still wishes to appeal. She is sent the decision in a mandatory reconsideration notice. She can now appeal to the First-tier Tribunal.

Have you missed the absolute time limit?

If you have missed the absolute time limit of 13 months, you can still ask the decision maker to look at the decision again. However, they may refuse to do so – in that case, you usually do not have the right of appeal.

The decision maker only looks at the decision again after 13 months in some very limited circumstances. If this applies, a revision can be carried out 'at any time' – ie, there is no time limit. If such a revision is carried out, you will have the right of appeal. But for this to apply, there has to be a legal reason for looking at the decision again.

The main ground for getting a decision looked at again in this way is when there has been an official error. This is when the decision contains a legal mistake made by the DWP, HMRC or local authority. Although that can include the way in which the decision was made, for example failure to take specific evidence into account, a decision does not contain a legal error just because you disagree with it. Make it clear that you are making a late request for a mandatory reconsideration, that you believe the decision you are unhappy about is wrong because of an official error, and say what you think that official error is. In practice, the DWP may be unwilling to accept your request.

3 / Making an appeal

Box C
What is an official error?

The DWP, HMRC or the local authority can make an official error. This can be:

- a mistake about the law (but not if this is only because it has been shown to be wrong by a later 'Upper Tribunal' or court decision)
- a failure to take specific, relevant evidence into account
- a failure to pass written evidence it has received to the decision maker
- a failure to ask about something that is relevant (but they are not required to keep your claim under constant review)

If you have asked for the decision to be looked at again after more than 13 months and the decision maker refuses to do so, in most cases you will not have a right of appeal. However, if it is sufficiently clear from the grounds of your request that it is for official error (and not, for example, that you simply disagree with the decision), you can argue that you should have the right of appeal.

What the law says

Late mandatory reconsideration for official error

Usually, there is no right of appeal where mandatory reconsideration is refused after being requested more than 13 months after the decision was made. But there is a right of appeal following refusals where 'the substance of the mandatory reconsideration request' is for 'official error' – ie, as distinct from an argument that the decision maker simply 'got it wrong'.

Upper Tribunal decision, PH and SM v Secretary of State for Work and Pensions (DLA) [2018] UKUT 404 (AAC); [2019] AACR 14

Do you have a mandatory reconsideration notice?

A mandatory reconsideration notice is the letter from the DWP or HMRC informing you that a decision has been looked at again and the outcome.

The letter is sent to you by post, or to your online account if it is about universal credit. Not all letters contain the words 'mandatory reconsideration notice'. However, if you have received a letter from the DWP or HMRC confirming that you have asked for the decision to be looked at again and it has reconsidered it, this counts as a mandatory reconsideration notice and you have the right to appeal.

If the decision can be appealed, the mandatory reconsideration notice should say so. If the decision does not have a right of appeal, but you think it should have, HM Courts and Tribunals Service decides.

4. Is there a time limit for appealing?

Your appeal must be made within a set time limit. This is one calendar month. The time limit starts from the date the decision in the 'mandatory reconsideration notice' was sent to you. If you want to appeal a housing benefit decision, your appeal must be received within one month of the date the original decision was issued or, if you asked for a 'revision', within one month of the date the revision decision was issued.

What the law says

Time limits

The basic time limit is one month.

One month = one calendar month.

The absolute time limit for a late appeal is 13 months.

Rules 22 and 23 The Tribunal Procedure (First-tier Tribunal) (Social Entitlement Chamber) Rules 2008; commissioner's decision R(IB) 4/02

> **EXAMPLE**
>
> **Time limits**
>
> A mandatory reconsideration notice is sent to Ezri on 4 November. The original decision is not changed by the 'decision maker'. Ezri wants to appeal.
>
> The basic time limit for Ezri to make his appeal expires at 5pm on 4 December – one calendar month from the date of the decision in the mandatory reconsideration notice. His appeal must be received by 'HM Courts and Tribunals Service' by then.

This basic time limit can be extended by 14 days if the decision did not contain a written 'statement of reasons' and you request one within the month. However, in practice, this rarely applies as most decisions are regarded as already including such a statement.

Note: the appeal must be *received* within the time limit – it is not enough for you to have sent it in time.

Have you missed the time limit?

If you do not appeal within the time limit, you may be able to make a late appeal. There is an absolute time limit of 13 months in which to do this. This 13-month period runs from the date the mandatory reconsideration notice was sent to you. For housing benefit, it runs from the date of the original decision, or from the date the revision decision was sent to you, if a revision was carried out.

If you request a late appeal, state this clearly in your letter or on the appeal form. Include the reasons why your appeal is late. 'Reasons' are not defined in the rules, but could include things like illness, a lack of advice or language problems. Also include why it is important for the appeal to go ahead – eg, the strength of your case and the amount of money at stake.

3 / Making an appeal

> *What the law says*
>
> **Late appeals**
>
> The First-tier Tribunal decides whether an appeal can go ahead. It is not restricted in what it can take into account when making its decision. Only in a truly exceptional case can an appeal outside the absolute time limit be accepted. This will be on human rights grounds where the right to a fair trial has been breached, and the claimant has done all they can to appeal on time.
>
> *Rules 22(8) and 23(4) The Tribunal Procedure (First-tier Tribunal) (Social Entitlement Chamber) Rules 2008; Upper Tribunal decision, GJ v SSWP (PIP) [2022] UKUT 340 (AAC)*

The tribunal decides whether or not to allow your appeal to go ahead, not the DWP, HMRC or local authority. It is not bound by any special rules, but must ensure that your request is considered 'fairly and justly'.

If the decision maker does not object, your appeal is allowed to go ahead, unless the tribunal decides otherwise. It is unusual for the tribunal to do this. Even if the decision maker objects, the tribunal can still decide that your appeal should go ahead. The tribunal may write to you and give you a chance to comment, before making its decision.

In very exceptional circumstances (eg, if you did not receive the decision that you wish to appeal against), it may be possible to argue that you should still be able to make a late appeal even after the 13-month time limit. However, you must show that you did everything you could to appeal on time.

If the tribunal refuses to accept your appeal, it cannot go ahead. You can appeal against the refusal to the 'Upper Tribunal'.

> **EXAMPLE**
>
> **Requesting a late appeal**
>
> Ella received a decision, dated 21 May, saying that she was not entitled to personal independence payment. She disagreed with the decision and asked for it to be looked at again. Ella's request was received on 15 June. A 'mandatory reconsideration' was carried out, but the decision was not changed. A mandatory reconsideration notice containing the decision was sent to Ella on 9 July.
>
> After getting the mandatory reconsideration notice, Ella had an accident at home which resulted in her spending a short time in hospital. Because of this, she does not appeal until 2 September. This is outside the basic one-month time limit, starting on 9 July, but within the absolute 13-month period.
>
> Ella states on her appeal form that she is appealing late because her accident and hospital stay made it difficult for her to appeal within one month. She also explains that her appeal has strong merits and that her GP can confirm that she needs a lot of help at home and did so even before her accident.
>
> The decision maker at the DWP does not object to the appeal going ahead. The tribunal decides to accept a late appeal and to consider whether Ella qualifies for personal independence payment.

5. How do you make a valid appeal?

Your appeal must be valid. This means it must satisfy certain conditions. If your appeal is not valid, it will be cancelled and not allowed to go ahead. This is called being 'struck out'. To help ensure your appeal is valid, you can appeal online or use the official appeal form.

> *What the law says*
>
> **Valid appeals**
>
> To be valid, your appeal must:
> - be in writing (in English or Welsh)
> - be signed by you (or certain other people)
> - include certain information
>
> A solicitor can sign an appeal for a claimant. A representative who is not a solicitor can also sign an appeal for a claimant, provided they have written authorisation.
>
> *Rules 22 and 23 The Tribunal Procedure (First-tier Tribunal) (Social Entitlement Chamber) Rules 2008; regulation 20 The Housing Benefit and Council Tax Benefit (Decisions and Appeals) Regulations 2001; Upper Tribunal decision, CO v LB Havering [2015] UKUT 28 (AAC)*

Your 'representative' can sign the appeal for you if you give your written authority, but to avoid complications it is best for you sign the appeal if you can.

Do you have to appeal online or use the official appeal form?

You can make your appeal about most benefits online, via the official website at gov.uk/appeal-benefit-decision/submit-appeal. You will need your national insurance number, details of your representative if you have one, and, if you do not know the date of the decision you are appealing against, your 'mandatory reconsideration notice'.

Alternatively, you can make your appeal by downloading the official appeal form (Form SSCS1) and sending that in the post. The form is available at gov.uk/government/publications/appeal-a-social-security-benefits-decision-form-sscs1.

It is not essential to appeal online or to use the official appeal form. However, it is strongly advisable to do so, as it is the best way of ensuring that all the relevant information is included and is received by the right person. A local authority may insist that you use its official appeal form, although the decision on whether your appeal is valid is always made by the tribunal, not the local authority.

What information must be included?

You must include the following details.

- Your details (if you are appealing about universal credit and you are claiming as a couple, this also includes your partner's details), and those of your representative, if you have one.
- The 'grounds' of the appeal. This is a summary of the reasons why you think the decision is wrong. The appeal form usually has a large box to use for these details.
- The address where the appeal documents should be sent. This can be your representative's address, but check with them about this.
- Except in housing benefit appeals, a copy of the decision you are appealing. This is usually the mandatory reconsideration notice.
- Except in housing benefit appeals, any documents in support of the appeal which the 'decision maker' does not already have.

If your appeal is about housing benefit, although you do not need to provide a copy of the decision being appealed, you must still identify it – eg, by giving its date.

The official appeal form also asks for additional information, such as your national insurance number and whether you would like to attend a hearing. If you request a hearing, there are further questions about the arrangements – eg, the dates you are unavailable and if you have any particular requirements at the tribunal venue, such as a hearing loop or an interpreter. The official appeal form from the local authority in housing benefit cases may ask for similar additional information.

Further details can always be provided at a later date.

What should you do if you cannot include all the required information?

The tribunal clerk can ignore (or 'waive') things that are normally required if this would be 'fair or just'. So, for example, if you do not have a copy of your mandatory reconsideration notice, send your appeal anyway in order not to miss the time limit and provide as many other details as possible – eg, the date of the original decision, evidence that you requested a mandatory reconsideration and evidence that this was carried out. Ask the DWP or HMRC for a copy of the mandatory reconsideration notice, and send it once you get it. However, the clerk is less likely to ignore the fact that you have not included basic information, such as relevant names and addresses.

What are the grounds for your appeal?

The grounds for your appeal are the reasons why you disagree with the decision.

Your grounds do not need to refer to the details of the law, but they must state why you are appealing and show why you think the decision is wrong.

- Grounds do not need to be lengthy, but should be as clear as possible. Just indicating your disagreement is probably not enough.
- Try to identify the particular reasons why the decision is wrong.
- Send any evidence you have in support of the appeal that the decision maker does not have. Send this as soon as it is available, and keep a copy and a record of posting. If there is something obviously wrong with the evidence used to make the decision, such as an inadequate medical examination, say so. But you can still send in evidence after you have submitted your appeal.

3 / Making an appeal

> **EXAMPLES**
>
> **Grounds for the appeal**
>
> 'I am appealing against this decision because I cannot work due to my walking problems and arthritis.
>
> - I can't walk more than about 20 metres without having to stop because I am so out of breath, and after that I can only walk about the same again before having to stop altogether. I don't use a wheelchair as I have not been recommended one by my doctor.
> - Because of my arthritis I can't stand or sit for long before having to move about.'
>
> 'I disagree with the decision that I am not entitled to personal independence payment. I think I am entitled to the daily living part because of the amount of help I need during the day.
>
> I need a lot of help with things like washing and dressing, and with cooking and eating, and with dealing with bills and letters – several times a day. I need a lot of prompting and encouragement to do these things because of my depression and anxiety. The nurse who examined me at the medical did not ask me much about this.'

Where should you send your appeal?

Send your housing benefit appeal to the local authority that made the decision.

Otherwise, send your appeal to 'HM Courts and Tribunals Service'. Note that these addresses sometimes change. They are given on the appeal forms available at gov.uk. Check with HM Courts and Tribunals Service if you are unsure.

- Appeals about universal credit, personal independence payment or employment and support allowance: HMCTS Benefit Appeals, PO Box 12626, Harlow CM20 9QF

- Appeals about other UK benefits in Scotland: HMCTS SSCS Appeals Centre, PO Box 13150, Harlow CM20 9TT. If your appeal is about one of the Scottish benefits, see page 52.

Is your appeal invalid?

Only the tribunal can decide whether or not your appeal is valid. If the tribunal clerk thinks there is not enough information in your appeal to make it valid, they can ask you to provide more. If you used the official appeal form, it is returned to you for more information to be added. It is important to comply as far as possible with what the clerk asks for. Otherwise, the clerk may decide that your appeal is not valid and may cancel it ('strike it out').

If an appeal is struck out, it does not go ahead. If your appeal is struck out, you can ask the tribunal to reconsider the clerk's decision. Apply in writing within 14 days of the date you were notified of your appeal being struck out.

In housing benefit appeals, the local authority decision maker can return the appeal form for completion or request that further information be supplied. If it does this, the basic time limit for appealing is extended by at least 14 days.

If you do not comply with the local authority's request, it must forward the matter to the tribunal – only the tribunal can make the decision on whether your appeal is valid.

6. How do you make an appeal about a Scottish benefit?

The appeal rules and procedures for decisions about the 'Scottish benefits' are slightly different from those about other benefits.

3/ Making an appeal

> Box D
> **The Scottish benefits appeals process**
>
> - Step 1: receive a 'determination' (decision) about your entitlement from a 'decision maker' at Social Security Scotland.
> - Step 2: ask for the determination to be looked at again by Social Security Scotland. This is called a 'redetermination'.
> - Step 3: if you remain unhappy with the outcome of the redetermination, appeal to the 'First-tier Tribunal'. If the redetermination is not carried out within the time allowed, you are given a form to appeal.

You can challenge any determination about your entitlement to a Scottish benefit in this way. This includes a determination that you have been overpaid, because that is about the amount of benefit you are entitled to. However, at the time of writing, it was unclear whether you can challenge a decision to recover an 'overpayment' from you (eg, because it was caused by 'official error') in this way. This is because it is unclear whether such a decision counts as a determination.

What the law says

Challenging a determination

An individual must be informed of a determination of their entitlement and of the right to a redetermination and appeal (in a way that leaves them 'with a record of the information').

Section 40 Social Security (Scotland) Act 2018

If Social Security Scotland does not think that you claimed the benefit or requested a redetermination in the correct way, or it does not think you had a 'good reason' for missing the basic time limit for asking for a redetermination, you are not sent a determination or a redetermination about your benefit entitlement. Instead, you are sent a 'process decision'. You can still appeal against a process decision. There is more about these appeals at the end of this section.

3 / Making an appeal

What is a redetermination?

Before you can appeal against a determination about your entitlement to a Scottish benefit, you must ask for it to be looked at again by Social Security Scotland. This is known as a redetermination.

Note that when you request a redetermination, the decision maker can look at the whole of the decision again. This means the new decision can be different from the one that you have asked to be looked at again. The new decision could be less favourable to you than the decision it replaces. Although this is not a common outcome, it happens in some cases.

You can request a redetermination if you are the claimant or the claimant's 'appointee', or if you otherwise have legal authority to act, such as a guardian, legal factor or as the executor of someone who has died.

What the law says

Requesting a redetermination

An individual can request a redetermination of their entitlement to a Scottish benefit. The request must be 'in such form' as required and within the relevant time limit, although in any case within the absolute time limit of one year. The Scottish government may introduce a rule allowing an exception to the absolute one-year limit in 'exceptional circumstances'.

Section 41 Social Security (Scotland) Act 2018

When notifying you of the determination of the Scottish benefit you have claimed, Social Security Scotland tells you how to request a redetermination. Usually, you are sent a form or can telephone 0800 182 2222. Contact Social Security Scotland if you need the form in large print, Braille, audio or in a different language.

If you have hearing or speech difficulties, you can request a redetermination via Relay UK (18001 244 4000) or, if you use British Sign Language, via Contact Scotland BSL. These arrangements may vary, so check what you must do in the information sent to you by Social Security Scotland.

Your request must be made within a time limit. This can vary for different Scottish benefits. You are normally treated as being notified of a determination two days after it is sent to you.

If you miss the basic time limit for requesting a redetermination but your request is received within the absolute time limit of one year, the determination can still be looked at again if you have good reason for not making the request sooner. Good reason is not defined but could include things like being unwell, finding it hard to deal with letters or not understanding what you had to do. If Social Security Scotland does not accept that you had good reason, you are sent a process decision instead of a redetermination. You can appeal against this process decision.

> **EXAMPLE**
>
> **Good reason for a late request for a redetermination**
>
> Georgia applies for a Best Start grant but is refused on 1 May. She is treated as receiving the determination on 3 May. Her basic time limit for requesting a redetermination is 31 days from that date, so her request should be received by Social Security Scotland on or before 2 June. Because of illness, her request is not received until 6 June. Georgia explains this and, as Social Security Scotland accepts that she has good reason for making a late request and it is within the absolute time limit of one year, her request is accepted, so that a redetermination is carried out.

Once you have made a valid request for a redetermination, Social Security Scotland must look at the determination again and redetermine your entitlement. It must do this within a time limit, which varies depending on which Scottish benefit is concerned. If your request is not dealt with within the time limit allowed, you must be informed of this and will then have the right to appeal against the original determination – you are sent an appeal form.

When a redetermination is made, you are sent a 'redetermination notice' about the outcome, and an appeal form for you to use (or telephone number to contact) if you are still unhappy and wish to appeal.

How do you make a valid appeal?

When Social Security Scotland sends you the outcome of your request for a redetermination, it informs you of how to appeal. An appeal form must be sent to you, and if you appeal in writing you must return the form to Social Security Scotland. You can also appeal by phoning 0800 182 2222 and providing the required details. If you have hearing or speech difficulties, you can submit an appeal via Relay UK (18001 0300 244 4000) or, if you use British Sign Language, via Contact Scotland BSL. For adult disability payment and child disability payment only, you can appeal online at mygov.scot/disagree-decision/request-redetermination-or-appeal. When it has received your appeal, Social Security Scotland must pass it on to the First-tier Tribunal, and inform you that it has done so.

There is a time limit for appealing. The basic time limit is that your appeal must be received by Social Security Scotland within 31 days of your being notified of the redetermination (or that the redetermination has not been carried out in time). You are normally treated as being notified of a determination two days after it is sent to you. If you miss the basic time limit, your appeal can still be admitted by the First-tier Tribunal if it is received within an absolute time limit of one year. You must give reasons why you did not appeal sooner. If the First-tier Tribunal accepts that you have a good reason for not appealing in time, it can allow your appeal to go ahead. Good reason is not defined but could include things like being unwell, finding it hard to deal with letters or not understanding what you had to do. The Scottish government intends to introduce an exception to the absolute one-year time limit for 'exceptional circumstances'.

3 / Making an appeal

What the law says

Making an appeal

There is a right of appeal against a redetermination. An appeal must be made on a form (although this 'need not be a physical form'). On receipt of an appeal, it must be sent to the First-tier Tribunal. An appeal may be made within 31 days of notification of the redetermination (or that the redetermination has not been carried out in time), but if made outside that time can only be made with the First-tier Tribunal's permission. An appeal may not be made if it is not applied for within one year.

Sections 46–48 Social Security (Scotland) Act 2018

What information must be included?

To be valid, your appeal must include the following information.

- Your details and those of your 'representative', if you have one.
- A postal address or email address where documents can be sent. This can be your representative's address, but check with them about this.
- Details of the determination you are challenging and why you disagree with it.
- Whether you think there should be a hearing of your appeal.
- If your appeal is late, the reasons why you did not appeal sooner.

If it is impossible for you to supply all this information (eg, if you have no fixed address), you should still submit your appeal as soon as possible, and explain why it is incomplete. Arguably, the First-tier Tribunal can ignore (or 'waive') a requirement that you cannot satisfy.

How do you appeal against a process decision?

You are sent a process decision by Social Security Scotland if it decides that you:

- did not claim in the correct way

- did not request a redetermination in the correct way
- do not have good reason for missing the basic time limit for requesting a redetermination

You can appeal against a process decision directly to the First-tier Tribunal – you do not have to request a redetermination first. Your appeal should be sent to the First-tier Tribunal at the 'Scottish Courts and Tribunals Service', not to Social Security Scotland.

What the law says

Appeals against process decisions

An appeal can be made to the First-tier Tribunal against a process decision. An appeal may be made within 31 days, but after that can only be made with the permission of the First-tier Tribunal. An appeal must be applied for within one year. The decision of the tribunal is final and is not subject to further appeal to the Upper Tribunal or to review.

Section 61 Social Security (Scotland) Act 2018

There is a time limit. The basic time limit is that your appeal must reach the First-tier Tribunal within 31 days of your being notified of the process decision that you wish to challenge. You are normally treated as being notified of a decision two days after it was sent to you. If you miss the basic time limit, your appeal can still be accepted if it is received within an absolute time limit of one year. You must explain why your appeal is late. If the First-tier Tribunal accepts that you have good reason for not meeting the basic time limit, it can consider your appeal. The Scottish government intends to introduce an exception to the absolute one-year time limit for exceptional circumstances.

Note that if your appeal is allowed, the First-tier Tribunal does not decide your benefit entitlement. Instead, it tells Social Security Scotland to determine your claim (or redetermine it). If you are unhappy with the resulting decision from Social Security Scotland, you can challenge that in the normal way – ie, by requesting a redetermination and then appealing if you are still unhappy. If your appeal against a process decision is refused by the First-tier Tribunal, you do not have a right of further appeal or review. Your only option for a further legal challenge is via 'judicial review'.

Your appeal against a process decision must be in writing. You do not have to use the official form, but it will help you to provide all the necessary information. The form is available from socialsecuritychamber.scot. Your appeal must be valid – and contain the information listed above. You can email your form to sscadmin@scotcourtstribunal.gov.uk, or send it by post to Social Security Chamber, Scottish Courts and Tribunals Service, 20 York Street, Glasgow G2 8GT.

Further information

For more details about getting benefit decisions changed, see CPAG's *Welfare Benefits Handbook*.

CPAG has a free elearning course about how to appeal decisions about Scottish benefits.

Chapter 4
Preparing your appeal

This chapter covers:

1. What are tribunals like?
2. Do you have a representative?
3. How do you prepare your appeal?
4. What is the point of the appeal?
5. How do you check the law?
6. How do you gather facts and evidence?
7. How do you write a submission?

What you need to know

- Tribunals are 'inquisitorial'. This means they are relatively informal and concerned with establishing facts and considering evidence in order to establish the truth.
- It is strongly advisable to have a 'representative' to help you with your appeal, if you can.
- Preparing for your appeal ideally involves your representative checking the law, gathering relevant facts and evidence, and writing a brief 'submission'.
- You do not have to submit further evidence or a written submission for your appeal, but doing so usually increases your chances of winning.

1. What are tribunals like?

Tribunals are courts of law. They are independent, they must apply the law and they must have a judge with legal expertise (or for appeals about 'Scottish benefits', a legal member). The tribunal asks questions, considers the evidence, establishes the facts and then applies the relevant law.

What the law says

The nature of tribunals

The overriding objective is to ensure that cases are dealt with 'fairly and justly'. This includes 'avoiding unnecessary formality and seeking flexibility in the proceedings' and 'ensuring, so far as practicable, that the parties are able to participate fully in the proceedings'.

Rule 2 The Tribunal Procedure (First-tier Tribunal) (Social Entitlement Chamber) Rules 2008; Schedule rule 2 The First-tier Tribunal for Scotland Social Security Chamber (Procedure) Regulations 2018

The tribunal that decides your appeal is the 'First-tier Tribunal'. Although the tribunal is a court of law, it is different from most other courts, such as a criminal court. These have an 'adversarial' nature, where cross-examination may take place and one side may have to prove its case 'beyond reasonable doubt'. None of those apply to tribunals considering benefit appeals.

A First-tier Tribunal has an 'inquisitorial' role. It is often more concerned with establishing the facts and considering the strengths and weaknesses of the evidence than with detailed legal arguments – although it must always apply the law. The 'hearing' is like a discussion or inquiry, rather than a conflict between two opposing sides, arguing 'for' and 'against'. The tribunal itself does most of the questioning, and there is rarely any cross-examination. There is no requirement to prove your case beyond reasonable doubt. The test (called the 'standard of proof') is simply whether, on 'the balance of probability', it is more likely to be true than not.

A tribunal hearing is therefore not as formal or potentially intimidating as a criminal or other adversarial court. The judge does not wear a judicial wig or gown, there is no dock or witness stand and other lawyers are not usually present. Usually, oaths are not taken, although the tribunal may require this in some cases.

A tribunal's main objective is to deal with cases fairly and justly. This is the case whether or not the appeal is decided at a hearing. There is more information about how your appeal is decided in Chapter 6.

> Box A
> **Appeals about Scottish benefits**
>
> If your appeal is about one of the Scottish benefits, the tribunal that decides your appeal is very similar to the tribunal that decides appeals about other benefits. Although some of the rules and procedures differ slightly, tribunals deciding appeals about Scottish benefits have the same overriding objective and role as other tribunals and operate in much the same way.

2. Do you have a representative?

When you have appealed, you are one of the 'parties' to the appeal. As a party to the appeal, you have a right to be represented by someone. A 'representative' does not have to be a lawyer. Most representatives are not legally qualified but still have expertise in benefits, and work in advice centres, local authority welfare rights offices or law centres. The organisation that made the decision you are appealing against (eg, the DWP) is also a party to the appeal, and has the right to be represented.

You do not have to have a representative, but it is strongly advisable, as they can help prepare your appeal.

Your representative's name and address should be notified to the tribunal. The tribunal can, if it wishes, still allow someone who has not been notified to represent. A representative has the same rights and responsibilities as a party to the appeal. This means they must help the tribunal to deal with the case and must co-operate with it.

What the law says

> **Representatives**
>
> A party to the appeal may appoint a representative (whether a legal representative or not) to represent them.
>
> Once notified, a representative is assumed to be authorised to represent, and they must be sent any document which the person they are representing should be sent.
>
> Parties to the appeal must help the tribunal to meet its overriding objective of dealing with cases fairly and justly, and generally co-operate with the tribunal.
>
> *Rules 2 and 11 The Tribunal Procedure (First-tier Tribunal) (Social Entitlement Chamber) Rules 2008; Schedule rules 2 and 9 The First-tier Tribunal for Scotland Social Security Chamber (Procedure) Regulations 2018*

Once you have notified the tribunal that you have a representative, they are assumed to be acting for you, unless you notify it in writing that this is no longer the case.

Your representative should be sent any documents about your appeal.

You may be assisted by someone other than a representative – such as a companion or relative – who is there to help you with practical or emotional matters rather than play an official role in putting your case to the tribunal. In an appeal about a 'Scottish benefit', this person may be referred to as a 'supporter'. Although you have the right to be assisted by such a person, they do not have the same role or rights as a representative. If someone is helping you as a companion or supporter, make it clear to the tribunal that they are acting in such a role rather than as your representative.

What is the representative's role?

There are not many rules about representatives and their role. However, there is general agreement about what tribunals usually expect from a representative.

- A representative is not expected to be a legal expert. However, they are expected to know the case they want to make and ideally set this out in a written 'submission'. They should know about the rules involved with the issue in your appeal. Your representative is not just your companion.

- A representative should be able to say how the relevant facts and evidence support your case – eg, why the official medical report is inadequate or how the letter obtained from your GP is supportive. Tribunals often like this set out in a written submission.

- They are expected to have prepared you for the appeal 'hearing', so you know you will be questioned about the facts of your case – eg, about your illness and how it affects you.

- A representative should be polite and co-operative. In a hearing, your representative is expected to assist the tribunal, not attack the 'other side', and aggressive conduct is disapproved of. However, they should still be assertive in pointing out the strengths of your case and the flaws in the decision.

Your representative can assist you with your appeal whether there is a hearing or not. Your representative's role will be similar however your appeal is decided, including (if possible) preparing a written submission. But some particular considerations apply if your representative attends a hearing with you.

At a hearing, the tribunal is unlikely to ask your representative many questions, as it wants to spend most of the time talking directly to you. The tribunal asks your representative to summarise the decision you are seeking and why. They should be able to do this briefly and concisely. Tribunals usually prefer this in a written submission, ideally sent in advance of the hearing. **Note:** because the tribunal relies on your representative to state your case and the decision you want, this may mean that it does not consider things that your representative has not argued for (although it has the power to consider any aspect of the decision). However, the tribunal must consider any issue that is clearly raised by your appeal (eg, by the evidence in the appeal papers), whether or not you or your representative have raised it.

> **EXAMPLE**
>
> **The decision being sought**
>
> Jude's appeal is about personal independence payment. His representative says that Jude does not dispute the decision concerning the 'daily living component', but wants to argue for the 'mobility component' to also be included. The tribunal cannot see anything which raises the daily living component as an issue in the appeal, so decides not to consider it, and to consider only the mobility component. It can do this because, although the tribunal has the power to consider any aspect of the decision, it does not *have* to look at the daily living component.

The tribunal knows about the relevant law. So if your representative attempts to instruct the tribunal on the law, it may not be looked upon favourably in particular if the law is generally well known. However, most tribunals do not object to representatives mentioning the law or caselaw if it is not well known or is particularly relevant to your case.

Knowing about the law relevant to the appeal is still important in most cases, as it helps your representative to understand what facts are relevant and what evidence you may need.

3. How do you prepare your appeal?

There is nothing in the law that says what you must or must not do to prepare your appeal. However, to have the best chance of winning your appeal the following basic steps are advisable in most cases. A 'representative' is best placed to assist with these steps.

- Identify the 'point of the appeal'. What is your appeal about? What decision are you asking the tribunal to make?
- Check the law and caselaw that is relevant to the point of your appeal.
- Identify the facts that are important to your case and the decision you want the tribunal to make. If possible, gather further evidence that is relevant to the point of your appeal.

- Write a brief 'submission', setting out what you are asking the tribunal to do, and how the facts and evidence support your case.
- Ask for a 'hearing' of your appeal. The tribunal can ask you questions at the hearing about the facts of your case. Ideally, you will have a representative who can be at the hearing too. However, your appeal can be decided without a hearing in certain circumstances (see Chapter 6 for more about this).

Have you got a representative?

Your representative can help prepare your appeal, including gathering evidence, checking the law and writing a submission.

If you cannot get a representative, you can still try to prepare your appeal, using the above basic steps. If doing all this is difficult for you, try to focus on the following.

- Get further evidence to support your appeal if you can – such as a letter from your GP or another person who has provided medical treatment to you.
- Ask for a hearing of your appeal and attend the hearing, unless you are content for your appeal to be decided without a hearing (see Chapter 6 for more about this).
- Prepare to be questioned about the facts of your case.

4. What is the point of the appeal?

The 'point of the appeal' is the basic matter of what your appeal is about – the decision you are unhappy with and what decision you are asking the tribunal to make in its place. In most cases, the point of your appeal is just about one or two things.

Knowing the point of your appeal as early as possible is vital so you can start to think about which facts and other information are relevant, and what evidence to get. Also, once you are clear about what the point of the appeal is, you can narrow down your search for the relevant law and caselaw.

The appeal papers sent to you before the 'hearing' usually contain the history of your claim, claim forms, copies of decisions, as well as a 'submission' from the 'decision maker'. This is a statement of how the decision was made and what the tribunal may want to do.

> **EXAMPLES**
>
> **The point of the appeal**
>
> Jarrod has been refused the element for 'limited capability for work and work-related activity' in universal credit, because he is not considered to score any of the relevant points in the 'work capability assessment'. But he considers that he should still be awarded the element, because of the risk to his health posed by his severe and uncontrolled blood pressure. The point of Jarrod's appeal is to show that, even though he does not score sufficient points, having to look for work would pose a 'substantial risk' to his health and so the rule about that should apply. Comments made by the doctor who carried out the medical assessment and from his own GP, as well as the history of why he had to give up work, support that argument and Jarrod should refer to those in his appeal.
>
> Beth has been refused the mobility component of personal independence payment because she is not considered to have any problems in moving around. She has been awarded the daily living component at the standard rate, and she is happy with that. The point of Beth's appeal is to show that her difficulties with walking are such that she scores enough points in the test for moving around to qualify for the mobility component. Evidence from her physiotherapist may help with that. She does not want to challenge the part of the decision about the daily living component, so that is not the point of her appeal. Beth can submit to the tribunal that her award of the daily living component need not be looked at (although she needs to be aware that the tribunal can look at it if it thinks it is wrong).

The various facts, evidence and law involved in an appeal can often seem like a bewildering amount of information. However, try not to worry about this. Once you have identified the point of your appeal, you will see that a lot of the information is only background material that is not important and, in fact, only certain parts of it are relevant to the point of your appeal.

Think of all the information in the appeal as being like a pyramid, with a lot of background information at the base, some partly relevant material in the middle, but most of the directly relevant material occupying just the top part of the pyramid. The top of the pyramid is the part that relates to the point of the appeal. If you concentrate on the material relevant to this, the mass of information will not seem intimidating.

EXAMPLES

The point of the appeal

Sarina has been told that she is not entitled to universal credit as a single person because she is living with Sam as a couple. The DWP says it has information from a credit agency that Sam has had bills sent to Sarina's home address. However, Sarina says that Sam has not lived there for two years and, in any case, they were only ever friends. The point of Sarina's appeal is to show that she is a single person and is not living with someone as a couple. Sarina asks Sam to confirm this and to explain why the bills were sent to her address. She also sets out the facts that indicate that they are friends and not partners.

Remy is French and has been refused universal credit because he is a European national and does not have a 'right to reside' in the UK. However, he has been living in the UK since before 31 December 2020 (when Brexit-related changes were introduced), has pre-settled status under the European Union Settlement Scheme and, before falling ill, he worked part time and had a right to reside as a 'worker'. The point of his appeal is that the decision maker was wrong to ignore these facts – had Remy's residence before 31 December 2020 and work been taken into account, it would have led to a decision that he kept his worker status, and therefore his right to reside, during a period of sickness. He supplies evidence of his earnings and work history.

How do you identify the point of your appeal?

Look carefully at why the decision you want to appeal makes you unhappy. Why is it wrong? If you have a 'representative', they should ask you about things that may have gone wrong – eg, if you think you had a poor-quality medical assessment, or if you did not include enough information on your claim form or questionnaire.

The point of your appeal may be clear from the decision. For example, if you have been found not to have 'limited capability for work' for universal credit or employment and support allowance, the decision may state that it has been refused because you failed the work capability assessment and include a list of the points that have been awarded (and not awarded) in the assessment.

More information about the appeal is in the appeal papers that are sent to you by the decision maker. These include the decision being appealed, as well as copies of your claim forms, medical reports and the submission, including references to the law, from the decision maker. This information can help you identify the point of the appeal. However, as the appeal papers may not be issued until shortly before the appeal is heard, in practice, it is best to try to identify the point of the appeal before they are sent.

5. How do you check the law?

The tribunal knows about the law that is relevant to your appeal. The tribunal does not expect you to know about the law, and does not expect your 'representative', if you have one, to be a legal expert. However, it does expect your representative to know about the basic law that is relevant to your appeal. Most appeals do not involve complex legal issues.

When making its decision, the tribunal must apply the relevant law; it has no discretion to ignore or alter it. So it is helpful to know about the relevant law to understand what the tribunal can and cannot do in your case.

4 / Preparing your appeal

> **What CPAG says**
>
> **Checking the law**
>
> Social security law can sometimes be complex, and checking the law that is relevant to your appeal is an important part of preparation. However, many claimants have limited resources and have circumstances which make checking the law difficult. A good representative can check the law for you.
>
> If you cannot get a representative, you can try to check the basic law yourself, using the advice in this chapter. This could also help you to think about the sort of facts and evidence that are relevant to your case. But do not worry if you are unable to do this. If you do not have a representative, the tribunal should help in understanding your case and what the law says about that.

What is social security law?

Social security law comprises two main things.

- **Legislation**, such as Acts of Parliament and regulations. This sets out the rules. Acts of Parliament set out the main rules in numbered sections. Regulations set out more detailed rules. These are numbered and may have sub-paragraphs.
- **Caselaw**. This clarifies how the rules in the legislation should be applied – eg, what the meaning of particular words or concepts in the regulations should be. The most common caselaw is in the form of decisions made by the 'Upper Tribunal'.

The 'First-tier Tribunal' must follow the decisions of the Upper Tribunal. If an Upper Tribunal decision is considered to be particularly important, it is 'reported'. If an unreported decision conflicts with a reported decision, the reported decision is normally applied.

A decision made by a three-judge panel of the Upper Tribunal is given preference to a decision made by a single judge.

If you see 'UKUT' as part of a legal reference (eg, as in *ET v Secretary of State for Work and Pensions (UC)* [2021] UKUT 47 (AAC)), that means it comes from the UK Upper Tribunal, and so indicates a decision of the Upper Tribunal. If the reference also includes 'AACR', that indicates that the decision has been reported because it is a leading decision.

For the 'Scottish benefits', the Upper Tribunal for Scotland uses slightly different references in its decisions. You can identify one of these decisions because of the reference to 'Social Security Scotland' and the use of 'UT' in the reference (eg, *CD v Social Security Scotland* [2024] UT 12). Decisions of the Upper Tribunal for Scotland are only about the Scottish benefits.

In a few cases, caselaw is from the higher courts – the Court of Appeal, the Supreme Court or the Scottish Court of Session. These take precedence over decisions of the Upper Tribunal.

Before the Upper Tribunal was created, the judges who made the decisions were known as 'social security commissioners'. Their decisions are binding caselaw in exactly the same way as Upper Tribunal decisions.

Decisions of the First-tier Tribunal are not caselaw: they do not have to be followed by 'decision makers' in other cases, or by other tribunals.

How do you find the relevant law for your appeal?

The relevant law is that which applies to the 'point of the appeal'.

> **EXAMPLE**
>
> **The relevant law**
>
> Christopher appeals against a decision that he is not to be treated as having 'limited capability for work' in his claim for universal credit, because he has failed the 'work capability assessment'.
>
> His representative identifies that the point of his appeal is whether Christopher should score more points in the mental health part of the assessment and, if he does not score enough points, whether he should still be treated as passing the assessment because there would be a 'substantial risk' to his health if he is treated as capable of work.
>
> The relevant law is where the work capability assessment, including the mental health assessment and the points that can apply, is set out. For universal credit, this is at Schedule 6 of the Universal Credit Regulations 2013. The rule about substantial risk is in Schedule 8 of these regulations.

It is not usually necessary to look up the law about things that are not closely linked to the point of the appeal – eg, when you have to make a claim, the fact that a particular test can be applied to your claim or when a decision on your claim can be made.

To find the relevant law, do the following.

- Firstly, look up a description of the relevant law – eg, use CPAG's *Welfare Benefits Handbook* or Disability Rights UK's *Disability Rights Handbook*. If you have a representative, they may have a copy. Your local library may also have one.
- Next, look at the law itself. Legal references are in the endnotes of each chapter in CPAG's *Welfare Benefits Handbook*.
- The law can be accessed online. All the relevant legislation is at legislation.gov.uk.

- The law is set out and accompanied by commentary in Sweet and Maxwell's *Social Security Legislation* books and in CPAG's *Housing Benefit and Council Tax Reduction Legislation*. The tribunal has copies of these books in the tribunal room, and usually places a lot of importance on what the commentary says. The commentary indicates the key decisions in the caselaw and describes the main points.

- Check for recent caselaw developments using the Upper Tribunal website at gov.uk/administrative-appeals-tribunal-decisions (for the decisions themselves), the *rightsnet* website and CPAG's *Welfare Rights Bulletin* (for descriptions of the decisions).

- For recent caselaw from the Upper Tribunal for Scotland, see scotcourts.gov.uk/judgments.

- CPAG and other organisations may have useful publications and websites. For example, there is some information about benefits and help with preparing appeals at CPAG Welfare Rights (cpag.org.uk/welfare-rights). The Disability Rights UK website (disabilityrightsuk.org) has information about benefits for people with illness or disability, including about benefit appeals. Rightsnet has advice for advisers about personal independence payment at pipinfo.net and about the work capability assessment at wcainfo.net.

> **EXAMPLE**
>
> **Finding the relevant law**
>
> Fran's appeal is about her son Noah's entitlement to the 'care component' of disability living allowance.
>
> 1. Fran gets help from a representative at her local advice centre. Her representative identifies that the point of the appeal is to show that Noah needs frequent attention throughout the day and that the help he needs is substantially more than that needed by a child without a disability, so that he can get the middle rate of the disability living allowance care component.
>
> 2. Fran's representative uses CPAG's *Welfare Benefits Handbook*. She looks up 'disability living allowance care component' in the index and then reads the description of the rules. This helps her to identify the issues.
>
> 3. Fran's representative then checks the notes at the end of the chapter for the relevant law. Using the abbreviations that are in an appendix at the end of the *Handbook*, she establishes that the basic rule is in section 72 of the Social Security Contributions and Benefits Act 1992. That rule can be looked at on the legislation.gov.uk website.
>
> 4. Next, her representative also looks up section 72 in Volume I of Sweet and Maxwell's *Social Security Legislation*. Here she can see not just the actual rule, but also some commentary describing how relevant caselaw has interpreted it.
>
> 5. As a final check, Fran's representative looks at the Upper Tribunal website, the *rightsnet* website and CPAG's *Welfare Rights Bulletin* for any recent caselaw that might be relevant.

Does your appeal have complex legal issues?

Usually, appeals do not involve complex legal issues. Most involve just one or two legal points that relate to the point of the appeal, and the tribunal is usually more concerned with facts, such as how your illness or disability affects you. Also, the tribunal knows about the relevant law, so your case should usually concentrate on the relevant facts and evidence.

However, a few appeals do involve more complex legal issues – eg, if there is a question about whether a particular rule may be in breach of human rights legislation, some cases involving the 'right to reside' test, or whether the law permits a particular regulation to have been made. Sometimes, the caselaw that has developed around a particular rule may be complex.

What CPAG says

Complex legal issues

If you are not experienced in social security appeals and there is a complex legal issue involved in your appeal, you should refer the case to a welfare rights adviser or representative or at least get advice from such a person.

6. How do you gather facts and evidence?

Box B
Facts and evidence: general tips

- Do not assume that the 'decision maker' already has all the relevant facts and evidence. For example, they may not have contacted your GP or consultant for further medical evidence.

- There may have been mistakes about some facts – eg, an error in a medical report about how far you can walk. You should point these out – do not leave it to the tribunal to spot them. However, do not point out mistakes, such as simple spelling mistakes, just for the sake of it. Always consider whether it is relevant to the 'point of the appeal'.

- Allow sufficient time to gather facts and evidence. It can be time-consuming, but could be key to winning your appeal.

Once you have checked the relevant law, you should gather the relevant facts and evidence. Exactly what facts and evidence are relevant depends on why you are appealing.

What are the relevant facts?

One of the main jobs of the tribunal is to establish the relevant facts. For example, if your appeal concerns your disability, relevant facts may include:

- how far you can walk
- how long it takes you to walk a certain distance or complete a certain kind of activity
- what kind of help you need with daily activities

If your appeal concerns whether you are living with another person as a couple, relevant facts may include:

- how you view your relationship with that person – are they just a friend?
- whether you share household duties
- whether you share bank accounts and bills

EXAMPLE

Relevant facts

The point of Zhen's appeal is to show that she is entitled to the 'mobility component' of personal independence payment. The relevant facts are those about Zhen's ability to plan and follow a journey and to move around. Does she need help from another person when she is undertaking a journey? If so, what kind of help is this? How far can she walk, and can she do so in a reasonable time? Can she walk without pain or breathlessness?

The tribunal expects you to help it establish the relevant facts as far as you can. You should point out any errors or things that have been left out to the tribunal. If you have a 'representative', they should make sure that you both understand what the relevant facts are in your case. In particular, check the following.

- What happened when you claimed? Did you represent your facts correctly on the claim form? If your appeal is about your illness or disability, do you think the doctor who examined you got all the facts right?
- Claim forms and medical reports. Is there anything that is relevant, but which has been overlooked in the decision? Are there important mistakes in the medical report?
- The decision maker's 'submission' in the appeal papers. Is there anything included that supports your appeal? Are there important mistakes?

What evidence do you need?

Tribunals deciding benefit appeals do not apply complex rules about evidence. Unlike in some other courts, there are no rules about what type of evidence may or may not be taken into account. All kinds of evidence can be taken into account.

What CPAG says

> **Evidence**
>
> Evidence (eg, from your GP) can be very important in winning your appeal. However, sometimes it is difficult to get such evidence – eg, if your GP refuses to supply it. You do not have an automatic right to be given further evidence for your appeal, and you may be charged for it. The tribunal does not get evidence for you, unless (in exceptional cases) it considers that it is necessary for making a decision.
>
> A good representative may be able to help you gather facts and get further evidence – eg, they may be able to write to your GP or consultant to get a letter to help with your appeal.

You are not automatically required to provide more evidence to support your appeal. What you say does not have to be supported by other evidence ('corroborated') to be accepted, and the tribunal can reconsider the decision based on the evidence it already has. However, that does not mean that evidence is unimportant. Tribunals have to establish what the relevant facts are, and regard evidence as essential to that and in supporting the conclusions they reach.

> Box C
> **Evidence commonly used in appeals**
>
> - What you say at the 'hearing' (eg, in response to the questions put to you by the tribunal). This is often important evidence in a successful appeal. If you have a representative at the hearing, the tribunal does not usually want them to give your evidence for you, unless you are unable to do so. However, your representative is allowed to ask you questions.
>
> - A witness attending the hearing. This could be, for example, your carer or a relative, or even the person with whom you are alleged to be living as a couple.
>
> - Medical evidence, for example, from your GP or consultant, district nurse or community psychiatric nurse.
>
> - Evidence, such as a 'care diary', showing how the impact of your illness or disability varies over time.
>
> - Non-medical information from a social worker or a carer, friend or relative can be helpful supporting evidence (eg, showing how your illness or disability affects your daily life).

In practice, most tribunals look for more evidence, and getting it will help your case. So, get supportive evidence if you can and, if possible, send it in to the tribunal in advance. The more closely the evidence applies to the point of your appeal, the more the tribunal is likely to consider it relevant and important.

What evidence is important depends on what is at issue in your appeal. Bear in mind that the tribunal can consider any sort of evidence.

Chapter 5 has more information about getting medical evidence.

> **EXAMPLE**
>
> **Relevant evidence**
>
> The point of Harry's appeal is to show that his tenancy is not 'contrived' and is on a commercial basis for the housing element of universal credit. Relevant evidence that already exists and that Harry could submit as evidence includes his tenancy agreement. Also, he may be able to submit further evidence about the circumstances in which the tenancy was created, that he paid a deposit or rent in advance, and that he has a regular payment history.

Can the tribunal ask you for further evidence?

Although you are not automatically required to submit further evidence for your appeal, the tribunal can instruct you to do so. However, in practice, this does not happen in every case. If your appeal is about the effects of your health or disability, the tribunal may ask you to get medical records for the period in question.

What the law says

Tribunal instructions about evidence

A tribunal can issue instructions (called 'directions' or, in appeals about Scottish benefits, 'orders') about the evidence it requires, how it is given and whether an oath is required. It can exclude evidence not provided as directed or ordered, and can issue a summons (in appeals about a Scottish benefit, a citation) to a witness.

Rules 15 and 16 The Tribunal Procedure (First-tier Tribunal) (Social Entitlement Chamber) Rules 2008; Schedule rules 15 and 16 The First-tier Tribunal for Scotland Social Security Chamber (Procedure) Regulations 2018

The tribunal is more likely to direct the decision maker (eg, the DWP) to provide further evidence. You can ask the tribunal to do this if you think this is essential for the decision to be properly reconsidered.

> **EXAMPLE**
>
> **Direction to provide medical reports**
>
> Keira is appealing against a decision that she fails the 'work capability assessment' and so is not entitled to 'new-style' employment and support allowance.
>
> In the past, she has always passed the work capability assessment, and Keira feels she has not got any better since. However, the DWP has not included the medical reports from all the assessments that she previously passed in the appeal papers. Keira asks the tribunal to direct the decision maker to supply these medical reports, because without them the decision about her failing the most recent assessment cannot be properly reconsidered.

How does the tribunal consider the evidence?

The tribunal considers the evidence by 'weighing' it. This means it decides how much it can rely on each piece of evidence and whether (and to what extent) it should prefer one piece of evidence over another. It can discount some evidence entirely. For example, although what you say about your situation is evidence, a tribunal can discount it completely if it thinks what you say is improbable or contradictory, or it can prefer other evidence if it considers that it is more reliable.

What the law says

Weighing evidence

Tribunals must give proper reasons for preferring one piece of evidence over another. 'Formulaic' reasons (eg, for preferring the 'official' medical report) are not good enough.

Commissioner's decision CIB/3074/2003; Upper Tribunal decision, AG v Secretary of State for Work and Pensions [2009] UKUT 127 (AAC)

In weighing the evidence, the tribunal will pay attention to things like who has provided it, how relevant it is to the decision in your case, whether it is consistent with other evidence and whether it is consistent and plausible.

If you are disputing an official medical report, the tribunal may often give weight to medical evidence (eg, from a GP or consultant) submitted on your behalf. However, the tribunal should weigh the evidence according to its merits in your particular case, not assume that any one kind or source of evidence is always preferable. The tribunal should not assume that the official medical report is the best evidence available, just because it is the official report.

The tribunal should not assume that evidence is biased – eg, that your GP has supported you simply because you are their patient.

What the law says

GP's evidence

A GP is a professional person not forced by anyone to give one answer rather than another. They can say a claimant is exaggerating if they think this is the case.

Commissioner's decision CIB/14442/1996

Have your circumstances changed?

In most benefit appeals, the tribunal can only consider the circumstances that applied on the date of the original decision – ie, the one you are unhappy about. It cannot consider any change in your circumstances that occurs after this date, even if the change was before the 'mandatory reconsideration' of that decision. So the evidence must be about your circumstances that applied at the time of the original decision. If the evidence is not clear about those circumstances, the tribunal may decide to give it little weight.

However, this does not mean that the evidence must also have existed at the time. So, for example, a doctor's letter about your ability to walk should be about your ability to walk at the time of the decision being appealed – it does not matter if the doctor actually wrote the letter after this date. Also, events after the date of the decision, such as a fall, can still throw light on your circumstances at the time of the decision if your condition has not worsened. In appeals about 'Scottish benefits', the tribunal can consider changes in your circumstances that have occurred since the date of the original decision.

What the law says

Change of circumstances and evidence

The tribunal cannot take into account circumstances after the date of the decision under appeal, but can take into account evidence produced after that date, provided it is clear that it is about the circumstances that existed at the date of the decision under appeal.

Commissioner's decision R(DLA) 3/01

7. How do you write a submission?

A 'submission' is basically something in writing setting out your case for the tribunal. It highlights what you are asking for and how the relevant facts and evidence support this.

A written submission for your appeal is not strictly required, but it is a good idea to have one. It is usually written by your 'representative'. If you do not have a representative, the tribunal does not expect you to write your own submission (although you can still do so if you want to). There is no official submission form.

In practice, tribunals often find a written submission particularly helpful. This is the case even if your appeal is to be decided without a 'hearing'. If you have a representative, the tribunal will hope to get a submission from them.

Writing a submission and sending it to the tribunal in advance of the hearing is a good idea for the following reasons.

- The tribunal has a clear and concise statement of what it is you want from your appeal and the basics of your case.
- The tribunal and your representative (or you) can refer to the submission, so you do not need to remember absolutely everything at the hearing.
- If the submission is sent in advance, there is a chance that the 'decision maker' may change the decision in your favour without the need for a hearing.
- If the submission is sent in advance, the tribunal reads it before the hearing and it may help influence its thinking.
- Tribunals like written submissions. If you have a representative and they have sent a submission, the tribunal will think that they have been helpful and co-operative.

What should be in a submission?

There are no specific requirements for the content or layout of a submission. Box D lists the basic principles that a submission should follow.

> Box D
> **Basic principles for a submission**
>
> - It should be concise.
> - It should be set out clearly, with headings and numbered paragraphs.

- It should identify the decision being appealed, and give details of the claimant and any representative.
- It should begin with a **summary** of why the appeal has been made and the decision that is sought.
- The relevant **facts and evidence** should be set out. This should not be all the facts that have been gathered, just those relevant to the 'point of the appeal'.
- Reasons (sometimes known as 'submissions') **why the appeal should succeed** should be set out – in particular, why the evidence shows that the appeal should be successful. Sometimes, it may be more natural to set out the relevant facts and circumstances in relation to each of these submissions as they are made, rather than set them out separately as we do in the sample submissions below.
- At the end of the submission, brief mention could be made of any **law or caselaw** that is especially important to the appeal. In many cases, this is not necessary. The tribunal already knows the basic rules and caselaw that should apply. Caselaw only needs to be cited if it contains very similar facts to those in your appeal, or is a very recent and relevant decision and may not yet be widely known. Referring to the caselaw commentary in the *Social Security Legislation* law volumes published by Sweet and Maxwell is helpful, as the tribunal uses these books – if you have a representative they may have access to them. As a rule of thumb, most submissions have no references to caselaw, or at most just one or two.
- If a particular part of the decision is not being challenged, the submission should say so. For example, in a personal independence payment appeal it can say that you are happy with your award of the 'daily living component' and do not ask for that to be looked at, but would like the tribunal to look at the refusal to award you the 'mobility component'.
- More than one argument can be made. For example, if the appeal is about the 'work capability assessment', it can be requested that if the tribunal does not accept that a particular

'activity' in the test applies, an alternative activity should apply instead.

- Strong points of the appeal – such as supportive evidence – should be pointed out. The tribunal should not be left to identify such strengths itself. Things that you have already said, for example on your claim form, can be pointed out. Remember that the tribunal may well want to ask you questions about such things in the hearing.

- Important omissions or mistakes in the submission made by the decision maker, as well as in any official evidence, such as the official medical report, should be pointed out. The tribunal should not be left to identify such omissions or mistakes itself.

- When pointing things out in the appeal papers, refer to the relevant page or paragraph numbers.

Sample submissions

There are no rules on how a submission must be written but there is general agreement on the basics. Your representative may have developed their own preferred style and have a 'skeleton' submission which can be adapted to the facts of your case. The submissions set out below are suggested as a basic structure and ways of presenting content.

EXAMPLE

Appeal submission – work capability assessment

Carys Jones suffers from back pain, which affects her walking ability, and depression. She is appealing against a decision that she does not have 'limited capability for work' for the purposes of her claim for universal credit. This submission has been written by Carys's representative. The representative has been able to get a supportive letter from the GP which has been sent in and has been included in the appeal papers (the representative has also sent in the letter requesting the evidence from the GP, so that the tribunal can see what sort of questions have been asked). The representative also argues that Carys has 'limited capability for work-related activity' – ie, so that she should get an extra amount of universal credit on that basis, and not be required to take part in work preparation or work-focused interviews.

The submission first clearly sets out what arguments are being made (in the Summary). After setting out the most important facts and evidence in her case, the submission then sets out (in the Submissions) why they should be accepted, with reference to particular facts and evidence, which include the letter from the GP, the report of the examining healthcare professional, and Carys's own account including things she put in her UC50 questionnaire. Because the facts and evidence are what is most important in this case and the tribunal knows about the law, the representative has not thought it necessary to have legal references or cite caselaw. These may be more important in a case involving complex legal issues, but those are not the most common sort of cases.

At the hearing, the tribunal will make note of the submission, and ask Carys about things like her walking ability and how her depression affects her, both now and in the past. It might only speak to her representative to ask them to confirm the main points of the submission, and if they have anything else to add.

Note: at the time of writing, plans had been announced to reform the work capability assessment. These plans included amending the rules about mobilising and on 'substantial risk'. These rules commonly feature in these appeals and are referenced in the example below, which uses the rules as they were in 2024. However, it was not known when the reforms would be introduced or exactly what form they would take.

Submission

Claimant: Ms Carys Jones [Carys's address, telephone number and national insurance number]

Tribunal: [the tribunal reference number, hearing date and venue, if possible]

Representative: [name and work address of representative, including telephone number]

Date of decision under appeal: 3 June 2024

Date of mandatory reconsideration notice: 25 June 2024

1. Summary

1.1 Ms Jones appeals against the decision, dated 3 June 2024, that she does not have limited capability for work from 8 May 2024 in respect of her universal credit award. The decision was confirmed in a mandatory reconsideration notice, dated 25 June 2024. The appeal was made on 2 July 2024.

1.2 The decision is wrong because she does have limited capability for work on the basis that the following descriptors in the work capability assessment apply, with the result that her points score is at least 15, and so above the required threshold.
- *Cannot, unaided by another person, repeatedly mobilise 50 metres within a reasonable timescale because of significant discomfort or exhaustion* (descriptor 1(a)(ii): 15 points).
- *Frequently has uncontrollable episodes of aggressive or disinhibited behaviour that would be unreasonable in any workplace* (descriptor 17(b): 15 points).

Either descriptor in itself is capable of satisfying the threshold for limited capability for work.

1.3 Should the tribunal be unable to award the above descriptors, it is invited to consider in the alternative a combination of lower-scoring descriptors in Activities 1 and 17.

1.4 It is not submitted that a descriptor applies to give a sufficient points score for Ms Jones also to be regarded as having 'limited capability for work and work-related activity'. However, Ms Jones satisfies the conditions for that on the basis that, were she not so considered, there would be a 'substantial risk' to her health. This is due to a significant increase in her depression and a possible recurrence of episodes of self-harm. Should the tribunal agree that Ms Jones has limited capability for work and work-related activity, it would also follow that she has limited capability for work, even if the tribunal does not award her the points argued for in 1.2 or 1.3 above.

2. Facts and evidence

2.1 Ms Jones suffers from a chronic severe back condition and depression, for which she is treated by her GP – see the letter from Dr Smith on page 40 of the appeal papers. Dr Smith's letter is based on Ms Jones's circumstances at the time of the decision under appeal. These conditions affect her daily life to a considerable extent. She had to stop work because of them. She has had no improvement in her condition since the date of the decision under appeal.

2.2 In particular, Ms Jones reports (answers in UC50 form, pages 8–10), that her back condition means the following.

- It is painful for her to bend and straighten up, including on getting in and out of a chair.
- She has difficulty walking, to the extent that, although she may be able to walk up to 50 metres once, she cannot do so again for a long time (one to two hours, and frequently longer) because of the pain. Consequently, Ms Jones usually only walks these sorts of distances once a day at most.

2.3 Ms Jones also has depression, which is only moderately well controlled by medication (letter from Dr Smith, page 40). One of the effects of the depression is that she experiences irritability which increases with stress and leads to outbursts of verbal aggression. Ms Jones says that these occur once or twice a week, but can be more common, including in her former employment when subject to workplace pressures and stress. When this happened repeatedly while at work, Ms Jones reports that on two occasions this led to episodes of self-harm at home (answers in UC50 form, pages 20–22).

3. Submissions

3.1 It is submitted that Ms Jones scores sufficient points in both the *Mobilising* (Activity 1) and *Appropriateness of behaviour with other people* (Activity 17) activities to be awarded limited capability for work.

3.2 It is submitted that descriptor 1(a)(ii) is satisfied because:

- Ms Jones's own account is credible and is well supported by her GP who confirms that her walking ability is significantly impaired by her back condition. The GP also supports Ms Jones's account that aids (such as a walking stick or wheelchair) would not assist in repeated mobilisation as the pain would still occur, including using and getting in and out of a manual wheelchair (letter from Dr Smith, page 40). This evidence should be preferred to that of the examining healthcare professional, whose report does not address Ms Jones's ability to walk repeatedly (pages 35–36). Dr Smith has treated Ms Jones for three years and knows her well. This should be preferred to the official medical report as his evidence is based on a longer knowledge of her and a better understanding of her limitations.

- The official medical report is not good evidence regarding repeated mobilising, as the examining healthcare professional did not explore Ms Jones's pain and ability to repeatedly mobilise in any detail, but rather merely asked how far she could walk before she had to stop.

3.3 Descriptor 17(b) is satisfied because:

- Ms Jones's own account is well supported by her GP who says that her depression is 'only moderately well controlled' by medication (letter from Dr Smith, page 40). This evidence should also be preferred to that of the examining healthcare professional for the reasons given in paragraph 3.2.

- The report of the examining healthcare professional does not contradict this evidence. Instead, it simply shows no evidence that her history of verbal aggression was explored in any detail with her, and so does not address the issue. Ms Jones says that she does not recall any specific discussion about that.

3.4 Ms Jones should be treated as having limited capability for work and work-related activity, as otherwise there would be a substantial risk to her health. The tribunal is asked to consider:

- Ms Jones's account of the history of her verbal aggression shows that this was worse in her former employment. Ms Jones reports that it was during this time in her life when she self-harmed after especially upsetting episodes at work.

- There is no evidence that her condition has significantly improved. The evidence of her GP is that her depression is only moderately well controlled at present. Part of this control stems from Ms Jones not being subjected to the stresses of work or a work-related environment.

- There is therefore a substantial risk that if Ms Jones is subject to the demands associated with work and work preparation, her depression and verbal aggression would significantly worsen, with the possibility of a recurrence of self-harming behaviour.

4. Caselaw

No caselaw is submitted as especially relevant to this case.

> **EXAMPLE**
>
> **Appeal submission – personal independence payment**
>
> Ahmad Lateef has anxiety and depression. He gets universal credit. His health condition limits his social contact and, because of low motivation, he needs encouragement and support for a number of daily living activities. He gets help from his mother for some of these. His claim for personal independence payment was refused because, although he was awarded some points in the assessment for help with daily living activities, he was not awarded enough to give him entitlement.
>
> This submission has been prepared by Ahmad's representative. In the example, the points already awarded are agreed as being correct, but Ahmad's argument is that further points should also be awarded in other activities. The representative has not been able to get evidence from Ahmad's GP, as the GP practice has a policy of not providing such evidence. However, an excerpt of Ahmad's medical records has been provided, and Ahmad's mother has provided a written statement and is willing to attend the appeal hearing as a witness. The submission shows how facts like these can be addressed in an appeal submission.
>
> **Submission**
>
> **Claimant:** Mr Ahmad Lateef [Ahmad's address, telephone number and national insurance number]
>
> **Tribunal:** [the tribunal reference number, hearing date and venue, if possible]
>
> **Representative:** [name and work address of representative, including telephone number]
>
> **Date of decision under appeal:** 8 May 2024
>
> **Date of mandatory reconsideration notice:** 28 August 2024
>
> **1. Summary**
>
> 1.1 Mr Lateef appeals against the decision of 8 May 2024 that he is not entitled to personal independence payment (PIP) from his

date of claim on 19 March 2024. Mr Lateef was awarded a total of 4 points by the decision maker. Although those points are accepted as correct, it is submitted that further points should be awarded. The decision was confirmed in a mandatory reconsideration notice of 28 August 2024. The appeal was made on 11 September 2024.

1.2 Mr Lateef submits that he is entitled to the standard rate of the daily living component. That is on the basis that he scores a total of 10 points (ie, at or above the threshold 8 points for the standard rate). He does not submit that he is entitled to the mobility component.

1.3 Mr Lateef submits that he is entitled to the following points:

Descriptor 4(c): Needs supervision or prompting to be able to wash (2 points – already awarded by the decision maker and not disputed in this appeal)

Descriptor 6(c)(ii): Needs prompting or assistance to be able to select appropriate clothing (2 points – already awarded by the decision maker and not disputed in this appeal)

Descriptor 1(d): Needs prompting to be able to either prepare or cook a simple meal (2 points – not awarded by decision maker)

Descriptor 9(b): Needs prompting to be able to engage with other people (2 points – not awarded by decision maker)

Descriptor 10(b): Needs prompting or assistance to be able to make complex budgeting decisions (2 points – not awarded by decision maker)

2. Facts and evidence

2.1 Mr Lateef has anxiety and depression. He has had these conditions for a number of years. They affect his everyday life in many ways, but in particular mean that he can become distracted by anxious thoughts and lacks motivation. He is assessed as unable to work for his award of universal credit.

2.2 Mr Lateef's mental health conditions seriously affect his ability to cope with domestic tasks such as washing and bathing, dressing and cooking. In addition, they have affected his social life considerably, as he finds it difficult to interact with other people. Also, because of these conditions, he has difficulty with financial tasks such as managing bills, planning finances for the month ahead and managing his bank account. His mother provides help with these things as best she can, by providing prompts and encouragement.

2.3 Mr Lateef is treated by his GP for anxiety and depression. He is prescribed an anti-depressant (citalopram). About two years ago, he was referred for a course of CBT which he attended as best he could, although his attendance was erratic because of his problems with motivation and social interaction. These treatments are summarised in the extracts from his medical records, which Mr Lateef has obtained and submitted to the tribunal to help with his appeal (pages 30–35 of the appeal bundle).

2.4 As Mr Lateef's representative, I asked his GP for specific evidence commenting on his reported problems in the activities of the PIP assessment that Mr Lateef contends for in his appeal. Unfortunately, the GP practice has a policy of not providing evidence for patients. It has not therefore been possible for Mr Lateef to provide his own medical evidence beyond the extracts from his medical records.

2.5 Mr Lateef's mother supports his appeal and has set out her evidence in a statement (attached to this submission). She will attend the hearing to answer questions about that evidence. The tribunal is respectfully invited to question her as a witness at the hearing.

3. Submissions

3.1 The available evidence, including the report of the examining healthcare professional and the extracts from Mr Lateef's medical records, clearly shows that Mr Lateef's mental health conditions are serious and long-standing. There is no evidence of significant worsening (or of improvement) since the date of the decision under appeal.

3.2 Regarding the points already awarded by the decision maker (for descriptors 4(c) and 6(c)(ii), totalling 4 points), these are accepted as correct by both parties and are therefore not an issue raised by the appeal.

3.3 The additional points contended for by Mr Lateef are 2 points for each of descriptors 1(d), 9(b) and 10(b). It is submitted that these additional 6 points should be added to the existing score, so that Mr Lateef scores a total of 10 points and is therefore entitled to the standard rate of the daily living component.

3.4 Regarding descriptor 1(d), Mr Lateef reports that his depression means that he lacks the motivation to cook and prepare a simple meal without prompting, often feeling that he will do without, eat a sandwich or get food from the local chip shop (PIP claim form, pages 6–8). He rarely eats three proper meals a day. Mr Lateef's mother says that she helps, usually daily in the evenings, by prompting and encouraging him to try preparing something for himself.

3.5 Mr Lateef tells us that although he had indicated that he sometimes has problems in this activity on his PIP claim form (see his answers at page 10), at the medical examination the examining healthcare professional merely asked if he was eating OK and was able to cook, to which he answered that he was. However, he was not prompted to expand on what that meant and did not explain that he lacks the motivation to cook. The tribunal is invited to ask Mr Lateef about this at the hearing. It is respectfully suggested that the evidence of Mr Lateef and his mother is better informed and more detailed on this point.

3.6 Regarding descriptor 9(b), Mr Lateef reports that he feels increased anxiety in many social situations and that associated low mood often deters him from socialising (PIP claim form, page 15). He tells us that he does attend his GP surgery for appointments and also his dentist annually, and that he goes to a local newsagent and the chip shop every week. However, he often needs prompting to do some of this by his mother, and he limits his interactions to answering questions and placing orders. The tribunal is invited to ask Mr Lateef about this at the hearing.

It is submitted that this level of activity does not amount to engaging with other people, at least without prompting.

3.7 Again, the examining healthcare professional's report does not indicate any exploration of under what circumstances Mr Lateef can do things like going to the newsagent and what happens when he does so, and so there is poor evidence to support the refusal to award points for this activity.

3.8 Regarding descriptors 10b, Mr Lateef reports that his anxiety disrupts his ability to deal with financial tasks such as paying bills, putting money aside for future expenses and arranging direct debits (PIP claim form, page 17). His mother says that she assists him with such matters. He tells us that although he has a bank account, because of his anxiety and low mood, he rarely checks it and relies on his mother to do that and report to him as required. The tribunal is invited to ask Mr Lateef about this at the hearing.

3.9 The examining healthcare professional appears simply to have assumed that because Mr Lateef has a bank account and is responsible for bills that little or no help is required. Again, this is poor evidence to support a refusal of points, and it is respectfully submitted that Mr Lateef's own evidence should be preferred.

4. Caselaw

No caselaw is submitted as especially relevant to this case.

Further information

If you are an adviser or representative and your client's appeal involves complex legal issues, you can contact CPAG's advice service for further help. This is not for people dealing with their own benefits claim – get help first from an adviser or representative at a local advice centre. See cpag.org.uk/support-advisers for more information.

CPAG runs training courses which may help advisers working on appeals. See cpag.org.uk/training for more information.

Chapter 5
Appeals about illness and disability

This chapter covers:

1. What problems may arise?
2. Medical evidence
3. What can the tribunal do?
4. How can you increase your chances of winning your appeal?

What you need to know

- Appeals about illness and disability are similar to other appeals. However, particular problems sometimes arise.
- Medical evidence is often important in these appeals, but there can be problems getting this and using it at the tribunal.
- The tribunal cannot take into account any changes in your circumstances that occur after you have appealed, including if your condition has got worse.
- The tribunal can use evidence from another of your benefit claims. It can also decide to make a decision that is less favourable to you than the one you appealed against.

1. What problems may arise?

Many appeals are about illness or disability. In particular, many appeals are about the 'work capability assessment', used to decide whether you are too ill to work or to plan for a return to work for universal credit and employment and support allowance, and the disability tests used to decide if you are entitled to personal independence payment (or, in Scotland, adult disability payment).

> Box A
> **The work capability assessment**
>
> The work capability assessment is the test used to decide whether you have 'limited capability for work' – ie, whether you are currently unable to work. The test is used to decide whether certain conditions apply to your universal credit – eg, whether because of your health you are expected to look for work or can have the 'benefit cap' applied to your entitlement. It is also used to decide your entitlement to employment and support allowance. The assessment normally involves your completing a questionnaire and attending a medical examination.
>
> The work capability assessment also tests whether you have 'limited capability for work-related activity'. This is to identify whether your illness or disability is so serious that you should not be expected to plan returning to work. If you are assessed as having limited capability for work-related activity, you are not required to plan returning to work, and can get the 'limited capability for work-related activity element' in your universal credit, or you get the 'support component' of employment and support allowance.

If your appeal is about your illness or disability, the main rules about how the tribunal deals with your appeal are the same as for any other appeal. However, problems sometimes arise, including the following.

- Getting medical evidence. Your doctor may refuse to supply further evidence or want to charge you for supplying it.
- Considering medical evidence. The tribunal may want to automatically prefer the official medical report, or give the medical evidence from your doctor little 'weight'.

- The tribunal cannot take into account any changes in your circumstances while you are waiting for your appeal to be heard, even if your condition gets worse.
- The tribunal may want to make a decision that is less favourable to you than the one you appealed against.

2. Medical evidence

You are not automatically required to get further medical evidence for your appeal. However, in practice, it is best to obtain additional medical evidence if you can, as it may increase your chances of winning your appeal.

What CPAG says

Getting further evidence

Although the tribunal has knowledge of medical matters and disability, it does not conduct a medical examination (unless your appeal is about industrial injuries disablement benefit). The appeal papers usually contain the official medical report so, unless you provide further evidence, there can sometimes seem to be an imbalance in the evidence that is available to the tribunal. Although further medical evidence is not essential to win your appeal, it is often important.

Your 'representative' may be able to help you get further medical evidence – eg, by writing to your doctor.

Further medical evidence is often a supportive letter from a doctor – eg, a GP or consultant. You can also get medical evidence from:

- an occupational therapist
- a physiotherapist
- a clinical psychologist
- a community psychiatric nurse
- existing medical evidence – eg, a previous medical report (UC85 or ESA85), when you passed the 'work capability assessment'

Sometimes, evidence from people who are not medically qualified may also be relevant – eg, social workers or care workers.

Has your doctor refused to provide medical evidence?

Your doctor is under no obligation to provide you with medical evidence for your appeal. Doctors must supply information to the 'decision maker' if they are requested to do so, but not to you or your representative. You are entitled to a copy of your medical records (see Box C), but usually this is not as helpful as a letter from your doctor directly addressing the issues in your appeal.

In practice, workload and other pressures (including information from the DWP emphasising that they do not have to supply evidence to claimants) has led to an increasing number of doctors, especially GPs, refusing to supply evidence. Some GP practices have a blanket policy of refusing to supply such evidence. If your doctor refuses to supply evidence to you, you can:

- try to persuade them to provide the evidence (see Box B)
- find other medical evidence to support your appeal (see Box C)

> Box B
> **Persuading your doctor to provide evidence**
>
> - Make sure your doctor knows that the very point of an appeal is that something may have gone wrong with the official medical assessment and that the tribunal must consider the accuracy of the official medical report.
> - Emphasise that you only need a short letter, not a lengthy medical report.
> - Point out that your doctor may have much better knowledge of you than the health professional who carried out the official medical, who has only examined you once.
> - Highlight that many appeals are successful.

If your doctor does supply supportive evidence, thank them and let them know the outcome of your appeal.

If your doctor cannot be persuaded to supply further medical evidence, other medical evidence may already exist.

> Box C
> **Finding other medical evidence**
>
> - Ask your doctor for a copy of your GP records that are held electronically. You may be charged for this.
> - Is there medical evidence in the appeal papers that supports your appeal – eg, a copy of a previous medical report in which you passed the work capability assessment?
> - Did you have a medical assessment? If so, and there is a previous official medical report that is still relevant because your condition has not changed but which is not already in the appeal papers, the DWP can be instructed by the tribunal to include it, as otherwise the hearing may not be fair.
> - Is there a medical report produced for another benefit that you have claimed that may be relevant? In particular, medical reports from personal independence payment claims may be used as evidence in employment and support allowance appeals, and vice versa. They must be relevant and used with care, bearing in mind that the benefits have different rules.
> - Do you have an occupational therapy assessment or a social worker's report that may be helpful?
> - The tribunal could get further medical evidence, if it considers that this is necessary for its decision. However, it is rare for a tribunal to do this as it usually already has the medical evidence. If it does get further medical evidence, this is not necessarily from your doctor – it could be from the DWP. You are not charged for this.

Alternatively, medical evidence may have been produced about another matter that is relevant to your appeal. This evidence is not usually as useful for your appeal as a letter from your doctor, but it may still be helpful.

What the law says

Previous medical reports

A tribunal is not always obliged to consider previous medical reports. However, it should do so where relevant, or where a claimant says there has been no change in their medical condition or disablement and that the evidence is relevant.

Upper Tribunal decision, FN v Secretary of State for Work and Pensions [2015] UKUT 670 (AAC)

Is there a charge?

Your doctor may be willing to provide you with further medical evidence, but may wish to charge you for it. There is no rule preventing this, or limiting the amount that your doctor can charge. You may pay the charge if you are able and willing to do so.

It is unlikely that your representative will be able to pay for you.

If you cannot afford to pay, consider the following.

- Emphasise to your doctor that you have been refused benefit and cannot afford to pay.
- Make it clear that your representative is unable to pay.
- Emphasise that you only need a short letter, not a lengthy medical report.
- In Scotland, legal aid may be able to pay for the evidence, if you are eligible. Your representative may be able to help you apply.

> **What CPAG says**
>
> **Charging for medical evidence**
>
> Your representative could consider liaising with your GP and other local doctors, by, for example, arranging a meeting at a local medical centre, to explain the importance of their support with appeals. This could be done in collaboration with people working on appeals in other organisations. In response to such liaison, some GPs have reduced their charges, or dropped them altogether.

How do you ask for medical evidence?

To be given 'weight' by the tribunal, your medical evidence should focus on what is relevant to your appeal. A diagnosis and list of treatments is less useful than a letter stating how you are affected by your condition, ideally referring to the point of the appeal. However, it is best to make it clear that you are asking the doctor to express their own opinion. You should not attempt to pressurise your doctor into giving the evidence you want. If you have a representative, they may be experienced in requesting evidence for an appeal.

- Ask for a short letter focusing on the point of the appeal, rather than more general information.

- Ask 'open' questions, asking for the doctor's own view, rather than 'closed' or leading questions simply asking the doctor to agree with what you say, or giving them the answer that you want. An example of an open question is: 'The tribunal will be considering whether the following statements can be applied. Can you comment?' An example of a closed or leading question is: 'Can you confirm that I cannot walk more than 20 metres?'

- Ask for brief reasons for the opinion your doctor gives. If the evidence is in the form of an opinion only, it may be given less weight.

- Ensure the evidence relates to your abilities at the time of the original decision being appealed. The tribunal cannot take into

account any changes since that date, even if the change was before the date of the 'mandatory reconsideration' of the decision. It does not matter if the evidence itself is produced at a later date.
- If your representative is requesting the evidence for you, they must have written authority from you giving your permission for the doctor to supply the evidence.
- When sending medical evidence to the tribunal, include your letter asking for the evidence, so that the tribunal can see what you said to the doctor.

> **EXAMPLE**
>
> **Letter requesting medical evidence**
>
> This letter is from a representative who is helping Carys Jones with her appeal.
>
> Dear Dr Smith,
>
> Re: Carys Jones, 12 Bevan Road, Splott, Cardiff
>
> Date of birth: 3 March 1970
>
> We are writing on behalf of the above who we understand is your patient. We include a form of authority from her.
>
> Following a medical assessment on behalf of the Department for Work and Pensions, Ms Jones has been held to be fit for work (ie, not to have limited capability for work) for the purposes of her claim for universal credit. With our assistance, she has appealed against this decision to an independent tribunal. The tribunal will reconsider the decision, and has the power to uphold it or decide that it should be changed. We are writing on behalf of Ms Jones to ask if you could provide a short letter to assist with that.
>
> We appreciate that your time is limited. However, the tribunal will find a short letter focused on the relevant questions more helpful than a longer medical report.

Ms Jones tells us that due to her back pain she cannot walk very far and has to rest for long periods after walking. This means she only walks any significant distance once a day. She also tells us that due to her depression she can become verbally aggressive on occasion.

The tribunal will consider whether the following statements, taken from the official work capability assessment, applied to Ms Jones on the date of the decision (3 June 2024). The tribunal cannot take into account any changes in her condition after that date.

We would be grateful if you could comment on whether you agree or disagree that these statements may be applied to Ms Jones, with a brief indication of your reasons, or are instead unable to comment. A brief statement of any medication and treatment she has would also be helpful.

1. Cannot repeatedly mobilise (including using a walking stick, manual wheelchair or other aid which is normally, or could normally be, used) 100 metres within a reasonable timescale because of significant discomfort or exhaustion.

2. Frequently has uncontrollable episodes of aggressive or disinhibited behaviour that would be unreasonable in any workplace.

We will also be submitting to the tribunal that Ms Jones should not be required to undertake work-related activity (such as attending work-focused interviews), as to do so would involve a substantial risk to her health, in that her depression and verbal aggression may worsen. Ms Jones tells us that in the past, following such incidents at work, she self-harmed as a result. An indication of your view on this would be helpful.

Please be advised that as Ms Jones is on a very low income and our organisation has limited funds, neither she nor ourselves can meet a charge for supplying the letter. If you propose to charge, please contact us before proceeding.

Thanking you in advance for your assistance.

Yours sincerely [etc]

How does the tribunal consider the medical evidence?

There are very few rules on how a tribunal should consider ('weigh') medical evidence. It should make up its own mind about what should apply. It should consider each piece of evidence on its own merits, without assuming that one sort of evidence is automatically better than another. For example, a very short piece of evidence from a doctor that is general in nature may be given less weight by the tribunal than a detailed medical report that focuses specifically on the issues. Chapter 4 has more information about general principles that apply when weighing evidence.

Some tribunals have wanted to give more weight to an official medical report automatically, simply because it is the official medical report. Problems have also arisen when tribunals have taken a critical attitude to the medical evidence produced for claimants – eg, by saying that doctors have been asked 'leading' questions or are biased in favour of their patients.

Generally, such approaches are wrong in law. The tribunal should not assume that the official medical report is automatically correct and should not make any assumptions – eg, that your doctor is acting under pressure from you. Some of the caselaw about weighing evidence described on the next page makes this point. For the tribunal to be justified in deciding that your doctor is acting under pressure from you, it must give specific reasons based on the facts of your case.

If you think the tribunal's approach is incorrect, ask for clarification of why it is taking it. If necessary, refer to supportive caselaw. **Note:** if a tribunal bases its decision on an incorrect approach, this may be an 'error of law', which could be challenged in a further appeal to the 'Upper Tribunal'.

What the law says

Weighing medical evidence

The official medical report should not automatically be preferred to the claimant's own evidence.

Upper Tribunal decision, MW v SSWP [2016] UKUT 76 (AAC)

Holding that the official medical report must automatically be preferred to that of the claimant would fly in the face of the obligation of the tribunal to consider all the evidence.

Commissioner's decision R(DLA) 3/99

The tribunal may prefer the evidence of a GP who has treated the claimant over many years; in other cases it may prefer the evidence of a specialist who is skilled in the condition from which the claimant suffers. It may attach little weight to a 'terse' certificate from a GP.

Commissioner's decision R(M) 1/93

Tribunals should not give 'formulaic' reasons for endorsing the official medical report – ie, merely on the basis that it is 'expert' and by someone trained in applying the test.

Upper Tribunal decision, AG v Secretary of State for Work and Pensions [2009] UKUT 127 (AAC)

A GP is a professional person not forced by anyone to give one answer rather than another. The tribunal should not assume that the claimant is putting words in the GP's mouth.

Commissioners' decisions CIB/14442/1996 and CDLA/2277/2005

A claimant's GP is just as professional as any other doctor or healthcare professional who gives evidence to a tribunal and, save where a proper explanation is given as to why they would do this, should not be assumed to be a vehicle for repeating what the claimant has told the GP as opposed to offering the GP's professional opinion.

Upper Tribunal decision, BH v Secretary of State for Work and Pensions (AA) [2013] UKUT 241 (AAC)

3. What can the tribunal do?

Can the tribunal take a change in your condition into account?

The tribunal cannot take into account a change in your circumstances, including a change in your health, that occurs after the date of the original decision that is being appealed. This applies even if your circumstances changed after this date, but before the date of the 'mandatory reconsideration' of the decision.

If your condition changes while you are waiting for your appeal to be heard, there are two main consequences for winning your appeal.

- Any evidence produced for your appeal should refer to your condition on the date of the original decision. If this is not possible, it may be possible to argue that it does not matter – eg, if your medical condition has been the same for some time and is clearly not likely to vary much over time. Remember that it is only a change of *circumstances* that cannot be taken into account by the tribunal. It can still take into account evidence produced after the decision.

- Any significant change in your health after the date of the decision being appealed cannot affect the outcome of the appeal, as the tribunal cannot take it into account. This applies even if your condition gets much worse while you are waiting for your appeal to be heard. In practice, this is common, as it can take several weeks or months before appeals are heard.

> Box D
> **Scottish benefits**
>
> In appeals about the 'Scottish benefits', the tribunal may be able to take into account a change in your circumstances that occurred after the date of the original decision that is being appealed, although the rules are not clear.

What should you do if your circumstances change?

If your health changes while you are waiting for your appeal to be heard, get advice about how this affects your benefit entitlement.

If you are getting benefit, you have a duty to report any change in your circumstances that you might reasonably be expected to know might affect your benefit award. So if your condition improves in a way that might affect your benefit entitlement, you must report this.

You are unlikely to be penalised for not reporting a worsening in your condition. But if you do report it, you may get another decision increasing your entitlement. The more serious the worsening in your health, the greater the case for reporting it. In any case, if you do get a new decision following reporting a change in your health but you are unhappy with the new decision, you will need to challenge that in order to get it changed. This is because the tribunal deciding your original appeal cannot look at the new decision again unless and until it is the subject of an appeal.

Can the tribunal use evidence from another benefit claim?

Because a tribunal can take into account any evidence that is relevant, it can sometimes take into account evidence from another benefit claim or appeal. This is most likely if the appeal papers contain such evidence.

What the law says

Evidence about another benefit

A tribunal can consider medical evidence from an appeal about another benefit, but should do so carefully and bear in mind that different legal tests are involved.

Upper Tribunal decisions, LD v Secretary of State for Work and Pensions [2009] UKUT 208 (AAC) and DK v Secretary of State for Work and Pensions [2012] UKUT 254 (AAC)

You may have two appeals at the same time – eg, you may be appealing about the 'work capability assessment' for employment and support allowance and the way your disability has been assessed for personal independence payment. In this situation, your appeals are considered separately by differently comprised tribunals. If your appeals are being dealt with at hearings, ideally you and your 'representative' should attend both hearings.

What the law says

Evidence about another benefit

Evidence about a claimant's previous entitlement to disability living allowance may be relevant to an appeal about their entitlement to personal independence payment, but ultimately it is for the tribunal to make its own judgement about whether the evidence is relevant and whether to call for it.

Upper Tribunal decision, CH and KN v Secretary of State for Work and Pensions (PIP) [2018] UKUT 330 (AAC)

Box E
Appealing about more than one benefit: tactics

- Consider whether any evidence from your other appeal is useful – eg, is it a potential source of supportive medical evidence? If so, what are its strengths and why should the tribunal give 'weight' to it? If you want it to be considered, submit the evidence to the tribunal.

- Are there weaknesses in the evidence from the other appeal? Do you think that the medical examination in the other claim was of poor quality for some reason?

- Remember that the different appeals concern different legal tests and, if necessary, emphasise that to the tribunal.

Although your appeals are heard separately, evidence from one appeal can be used in the other – eg, if your appeal concerns your disability and how it affects you, some issues (such as your ability to walk) may be common to both appeals. The tribunal should ensure that you and the 'decision maker' can see this evidence and are able to comment on it. As the tribunals are separate, it is possible that they might take different approaches and arrive at different conclusions.

> **EXAMPLE**
>
> **Using evidence from another benefit claim**
>
> Simone's appeal is about a decision that she failed the work capability assessment for universal credit, and includes whether she should score more points for her problems with walking. She has also claimed personal independence payment and been awarded the standard rate of the 'mobility component' because of the difficulty she has walking. The tribunal can take any relevant evidence from the personal independence payment claim, including about her walking, when deciding her employment and support allowance appeal, but will bear in mind that the tests for walking ability for the two benefits are different.

Can the tribunal make a less favourable decision?

The tribunal can completely reconsider the decision being appealed and can also make whatever decision the decision maker (eg, the DWP, or in appeals about the Scottish benefits, Social Security Scotland) could have made. It can therefore make a decision that is less favourable to you than the one you appealed against.

This is the case, even if you have not specifically appealed against all parts of the original decision. The tribunal does not have to look at the aspects that you do not want changed, but it can if it thinks they may be wrong. If it is going to do this, the tribunal should warn you and, depending on the facts of your case, give you a chance for an 'adjournment' of the hearing to get advice or more evidence, or to consider withdrawing your appeal. The tribunal should still give you a warning even if you have a representative.

What the law says

Warnings about less favourable decisions

A tribunal should warn a claimant that it will consider reducing an award, even where the claimant has a representative. Although a tribunal can rely on a representative which it knows to be competent and experienced, even then there must be some form of indication given that the award may be reduced.

Upper Tribunal decision, LJ v Secretary of State for Work and Pensions (PIP) [2017] UKUT 455

A tribunal considering making a less favourable decision in an appeal from a claimant who is not represented should consider adjourning to allow the claimant to think about their response and seek representation, even if the claimant has not sought an adjournment: failure to do so could be a breach of the rules of natural justice.

Upper Tribunal decision, MS v Secretary of State for Work and Pensions (DLA and PIP) [2021] UKUT 41 (AAC)

Making a less favourable decision is most likely in some personal independence payment and disability living allowance appeals. This is because there are a number of things that concern your entitlement in the decision: whether you are entitled to one or both components, the rate you get and for how long. So an appeal about one aspect of the decision allows the other aspects to be considered too.

In appeals about the work capability assessment, it is less common for a tribunal to make a less favourable decision. However, the tribunal could, for example, reduce the total points score awarded to you, or even decide that you do not pass the assessment at all, even though you have only appealed against the decision not to place you in the 'support group' or, in a universal credit claim, the 'limited capability for work-related activity' group.

Box F
Avoiding a less favourable decision

- Is there an element of the decision on your claim that is at risk of a less favourable decision? For example, have you been awarded a personal independence payment component that you are happy with (and so have not appealed about), but which the tribunal might well want to look at because it seems quite generous?

- If so, consider whether it is advisable to continue with the appeal. Remember, the tribunal can look at all elements of the decision.

- If the tribunal indicates that it wishes to consider a part of the decision that you do not want changed, in particular if it is considering making a less favourable decision, it should let you know and allow you at least a brief adjournment. It may offer you the opportunity of a longer adjournment to consider the unappealed part of the decision, or allow you to withdraw your appeal. If you have a representative, the tribunal expects them to help you decide what to do.

- If a tribunal warns you it is considering making a less favourable decision, consider very carefully whether to withdraw your appeal. In practice, it may be difficult to persuade the tribunal not to make a less favourable decision if you decide to proceed with the appeal. Be careful about declining an offer of an adjournment to consider what to do. If you do this but then later wish to argue that the tribunal should have granted one, it will be very difficult to succeed.

If you have appealed against a decision that you fail the work capability assessment and the tribunal agrees with you and decides that you do in fact pass it, it should also consider whether you should be in the support group or, for universal credit, the limited capability for work-related activity group, as this is also part of the decision being appealed.

> **EXAMPLE**
>
> **A less favourable decision**
>
> Nathan receives a decision that he is entitled to the 'daily living component' of personal independence payment at the standard rate, but that he is not entitled to the 'mobility component'. Nathan thinks he should get the mobility component too and so appeals.
>
> However, after considering the evidence, the tribunal thinks that it may refuse his appeal about the mobility component, and also alter the original decision to remove his entitlement to the daily living component.
>
> The tribunal warns Nathan that it is considering this. If he decides to continue with the appeal, the tribunal has the power to take away the daily living component as well as to refuse the mobility component. If this happens, Nathan will lose all his personal independence payment.

4. How can you increase your chances of winning your appeal?

In many ways, appeals about illness or disability are no different from any other appeal. So, to maximise your chances of success, do the following.

- Request a 'hearing' of the appeal, attended by you and, ideally, your 'representative' (there is more about this in Chapter 6).
- Provide evidence that supports your appeal, for example, a letter from your GP or consultant.

There are other things that you can do to increase your chances of winning an appeal about the 'work capability assessment' or an appeal about your disability.

Work capability assessment appeals: is there a risk to health?

What the law says

The substantial risk rule

If you do not score sufficient points in the work capability assessment to win your appeal, you should still do so if there would otherwise be a substantial risk to your physical or mental health, or to someone else's physical or mental health, unless that risk could be avoided by reasonable adjustments.

Schedule 8 paragraph 4 and Schedule 9 paragraph 4 The Universal Credit Regulations 2013; regulations 25 and 31 The Employment and Support Allowance Regulations 2013; regulations 29 and 35 The Employment and Support Allowance Regulations 2008

If you are appealing against the outcome of the work capability assessment that decides whether you have 'limited capability for work' for benefit purposes, you can increase your chances of success by considering a rule that is sometimes overlooked. This treats you as satisfying the assessment if there would be a substantial risk to your (or to someone else's) health if you were found not to have limited capability for work. A similar rule applies to the test for 'limited capability for work-related activity'.

Check whether you can argue that there is a substantial risk, even if you are also arguing about the number of points that should be awarded to you in the assessment. You can argue that you should score enough points and that a substantial risk applies if you do not score enough points.

Note: at the time of writing, official plans to change the substantial risk rule had been announced. These plans included that for the limited capability for work-related activity test, the substantial risk rule would be changed so that it only applies to certain specified conditions or circumstances. However, it had not been confirmed if or when such changes would be introduced.

The substantial risk could be from doing the sort of work or work-related activity that you may be expected to do, or from travelling to and from work or the job centre, or taking part in interviews at the job centre. The tribunal does not need to consider actual job descriptions, just the kind of work that you might be able to do. Risks can arise from travelling to or from work.

What the law says

Substantial risk

In a case about limited capability for work, the tribunal should, when considering substantial risk, assess the range or type of work which a claimant is capable of performing in assessing the risk to themself or to others. That can include the journey to or from work or the job centre.

Court of Appeal decision, Charlton v Secretary of State for Work and Pensions [2009] EWCA Civ 42; commissioner's decision R(IB) 2/09; Upper Tribunal decision, IM v Secretary of State for Work and Pensions (ESA) [2014] UKUT 412 (AAC), reported as [2015] AACR 10; Upper Tribunal decision, ET v Secretary of State for Work and Pensions (UC) [2021] UKUT 47 (AAC)

If your appeal is about whether you have limited capability for work-related activity, the tribunal should have evidence about the kind of work-related activity in your area that the DWP considers you could do without incurring substantial risk.

> **EXAMPLE**
>
> **Substantial risk**
>
> Andrea appeals against a decision that she fails the work capability assessment and so is not entitled to employment and support allowance. She experiences anxiety and depression, and has problems coping with change and with social situations. In the past, her mental health problems have been severe and she has harmed herself.
>
> The tribunal decides that Andrea does have limited capability for work and therefore satisfies the work capability assessment, and so allows her appeal. Although the tribunal did not score her sufficient points to pass the assessment, it decided that if she did not pass the assessment, the pressures of a working environment would pose a substantial risk to her health. Her mental health would be affected and this may cause her to harm herself again.

Disability appeals: keeping a diary

If you are appealing about a disability benefit (eg, personal independence payment or adult disability payment), a care or mobility 'diary' can be a helpful source of additional evidence, especially if there are significant fluctuations in your condition, so that you tend to have good and bad periods. The same applies to your child's condition if the appeal is about a disability benefit for them (eg, disability living allowance or child disability payment).

The disability test for personal independence payment requires that a particular 'descriptor' (a statement describing your ability to carry out a number of activities) must apply for more than 50 per cent of the days in the one-year period taken into account when deciding your entitlement. There is no specific rule for disability living allowance and attendance allowance, but the test looks at whether you satisfy the disability test for 'most of the time'.

A diary, in which you record the level and frequency of your care needs or your walking ability over a period of time, can therefore help show whether you satisfy the test. When recording your walking ability, try to indicate not only how far you can walk (bearing in mind that distances in the law are given in metres), but also other relevant things such as whether you are using an aid (eg, a walking stick or frame), how long it takes you to walk as far as you do, and whether you need to stop because of discomfort or breathlessness and how long before you can start walking again.

You do not need to keep your diary in any particular form, but be as clear and as accurate as possible – eg, use a page for each day. Ideally, keep your diary over a period of time that most accurately reflects fluctuations in your condition. So, if you tend to have good days and bad days, a period of a few weeks is probably enough; but if you tend to have good weeks and bad weeks, you may need to keep it for a month or more.

Further information

CPAG's *Personal Independence Payment: what you need to know* outlines the assessment criteria used for personal independence payment, including the activities you are tested against and the points you must score to qualify for an award.
An example of a care diary to help with a claim for disability living allowance for a child is in Disability Rights UK's *Disability Rights Handbook*.

More information about supporting evidence is in Chapter 15 of CPAG's *Benefits and Mental Health Handbook*, free to access online at cpag.org.uk/handbooks.

Chapter 6
Deciding your appeal

This chapter covers:

1. What happens after you have made your appeal?
2. How is your appeal decided?
3. What happens at a hearing?
4. What happens after the tribunal has made its decision?
5. Deciding appeals about Scottish benefits

What you need to know

- Your appeal is decided either at a 'hearing' or by the tribunal looking at the appeal papers. You are more likely to win your appeal if you attend a hearing (which may be by telephone, video call or in person).
- Your appeal can be cancelled ('struck out') if you do not respond to queries from the tribunal clerk.
- Hearings can be 'postponed' or 'adjourned', but there is no legal right to this.
- There are no precise rules about how hearings are run, but there is an overall requirement to be fair.
- Most tribunals give their decision on the same day as the hearing. Some decisions may be given later in writing.

1. What happens after you have made your appeal?

After you have made your appeal, it may be some time (possibly several months) before it is decided by the tribunal. During this time, in most cases, your appeal is handled by 'HM Courts and Tribunals Service'. Your main point of contact with the tribunal before it is decided is with the tribunal clerk.

> Box A
> **Scottish benefits**
>
> If you have appealed about one of the 'Scottish benefits', your appeal is administered by the 'Scottish Courts and Tribunals Service'. The way these appeals are administered, handled and decided is very similar to appeals about other benefits, although there are some differences. There is more about this in section 5 of this chapter.

When HM Courts and Tribunals Service receives your appeal, it checks to make sure that it is valid. If it thinks there may be a problem, it may return the appeal for you to correct. Do not ignore this request. If you do, there is a risk that the appeal will be cancelled ('struck out').

If your appeal is valid, or if HM Courts and Tribunals Service thinks that any problems can be ignored ('waived'), it sends you an acknowledgement. This includes the contact details for the office handling your appeal. It may also include an enquiry form if it needs more details, such as whether you want a 'hearing' of your appeal, details of your 'representative' or if you need an interpreter.

A copy of your appeal is sent to the 'decision maker' (eg, at the DWP). They prepare a 'response' to the appeal, explaining how the decision was made. In housing benefit appeals, the decision maker at the local authority prepares a response and sends it to HM Courts and Tribunals Service and to you. The decision maker must make the response within 28 days (or for housing benefit appeals, 'as soon as reasonably practical').

The decision maker's response is included in a set of appeal papers – sometimes referred to as a 'bundle'. The appeal papers also include copies of the decision, relevant documents (eg, the claim form and the official medical report), further evidence provided since the 'mandatory reconsideration' stage and a 'submission' that includes a summary of the reasons for making the decision.

Is there a delay?

There may be some time to wait before your appeal is considered by the tribunal. Get advice about your benefit entitlement during this period.

If there is an urgent need for your appeal to be decided quickly, you can contact the tribunal clerk and ask for the tribunal to set an early date for deciding the appeal (known as 'expediting' the appeal). The tribunal clerk does not have to agree to this. Explain why an earlier decision is important in your case – eg, if your health is at risk or you may be evicted from your home, or your benefit is your only source of income and you cannot afford essentials without it. The clerk may decide to pass the request to a tribunal judge to see if the appeal can be decided quickly – there is more about this below.

Can the appeal lapse?

Once you have appealed, in most cases, the decision maker (eg, at the DWP) can still change the decision before the appeal is heard. If they do this and the new decision is more advantageous to you (even if it still does not give you everything you want), your appeal 'lapses' (ie, it does not go ahead), unless you renew it.

If you are contacted about this by the DWP, ask your representative for advice. Unless the new decision gives you everything you have asked for in your appeal, it is usually better to say that you still want to appeal.

If a new decision is issued before the appeal is heard, and you do not want your appeal to lapse, make sure you renew your appeal.

6 / Deciding your appeal

> Box B
> **Scottish benefits**
>
> At the time of writing, decision makers at Social Security Scotland did not have the power to change decisions before the appeal was heard. There were plans to change the rules so that this became possible at least in some cases.

It is not very common for an appeal to lapse. Usually, it only happens if new information or evidence is received before the appeal is heard. However, if your appeal is about personal independence payment, the DWP may telephone you to discuss the possibility of making a new decision, giving you at least some of what you want, so that your appeal lapses even without new information or evidence. See Box C.

> Box C
> **Personal independence payment and lapsing of your appeal**
>
> - The DWP may phone you to discuss making a new decision so that your personal independence payment appeal lapses.
> - Some claimants and their representatives have experienced the DWP making an 'offer' of a new decision so that you 'drop' your appeal. The DWP says this is not its policy. Instead, it says that if the new decision would not give you everything that you could be awarded by the tribunal, it will only make a new decision if you agree, and the call is to explain that.
> - If you have a representative, the DWP should contact them about this, rather than you.
> - You do not have to agree to a new decision being made. But you can tell the decision maker that you do want them to make the new decision and still appeal against it when it is made. If a new decision is made, your appeal will lapse, but you can still renew your appeal against the new decision (you do not need special reasons). This should be explained to you. If a new decision is not made (ie, because you do not agree

to it), your appeal against the original decision will not lapse and continues as usual.

- If your appeal goes ahead, or if you have renewed your appeal against the new decision, in general, the tribunal can still consider your entitlement afresh in the normal way. However, the tribunal must take the decision that the DWP proposed to make, or the new decision if they did actually make one, as the starting point for its consideration. If the tribunal wants to make a decision less favourable to you than the one the DWP wanted to make, it must give you an adequate warning so, for example, you have a chance to get advice or to make arguments about why a less favourable decision should not be made.

What the law says

Warning about less favourable decisions

If the tribunal is inclined to make a decision less favourable than the one the DWP has made, or wants to make, it must give adequate warning about that.

Upper Tribunal decision, DO v Secretary of State for Work and Pensions (PIP) [2021] UKUT 161 (AAC)

Can the appeal be decided quickly?

In some cases, the tribunal may look at the evidence in your appeal papers and contact you to say that it has reached a preliminary view of your appeal, and can make a quick decision without a hearing. This can also happen if you asked for your appeal to be heard more quickly (expedited), and the tribunal clerk passed the request to a tribunal judge.

You should not be pressured into accepting a quick decision or be given the impression that you are being offered a deal. The tribunal should make it clear that if you decide to proceed with your appeal at a hearing, the decision may be more or less favourable to you. If

6 / Deciding your appeal

you agree to the decision the tribunal is minded to make, the appeal is decided on the appeal papers, and there is no hearing.

If you are contacted about this, ask your representative for advice. Whether or not you have a representative, you should consider whether the tribunal is minded to give you everything you have requested, or at least that you have a reasonable chance of getting. Remember that at a hearing the tribunal will also ask you questions and will not be bound by any possible quick decision discussed with you before the hearing – ie, it can change its mind about the decision.

Sometimes the tribunal may discuss its preliminary view with you at the start of a hearing, having just looked at the appeal papers. The same advice applies to this situation as it does to when the tribunal contacts you about a quick decision before the hearing.

What the law says

Preliminary views of the tribunal

There is nothing wrong in principle with a tribunal coming to a preliminary view on the basis of the appeal papers. Where a tribunal shares its preliminary view with the parties to the appeal, it should do so in a clear language which does not put pressure on the claimant to take any particular course. Language such as 'offer' is not appropriate.

Upper Tribunal decision, KMN v Secretary of State for Work and Pensions (PIP) [2019] UKUT 42 (AAC)

There is more about the various ways of deciding an appeal in section 2 of this chapter.

Can you withdraw your appeal?

If you withdraw your appeal, it is not considered by the tribunal, and the original decision that you appealed against stands. You do not have to give any reasons.

You can withdraw your appeal by writing to the tribunal. If your appeal is not to be decided at a hearing, this can be done at any time. The withdrawal is automatic unless the tribunal directs that it must agree to the withdrawal. If there is to be a hearing of your appeal, you can withdraw your appeal in writing at any time before the hearing starts.

Once the hearing has started, you can tell the tribunal judge that you want to withdraw your appeal. But once the hearing has started (or it has been 'adjourned' and the tribunal has directed that you need its permission to withdraw), the tribunal has to agree to the withdrawal. In that case, you could be asked to give reasons.

If your appeal has been withdrawn, it can be reinstated by the tribunal. For this to happen, you (or the DWP, HMRC or the local authority) must apply to the tribunal in writing. Your application must be received within one month of the date the tribunal received your application to withdraw.

Can your appeal be cancelled?

An appeal can be cancelled (known as being struck out) by the tribunal in the following circumstances.

- You have not complied with a tribunal 'direction' which warned you that being struck out was a possibility if you did not comply – eg, you have not supplied information it has requested. Your appeal is cancelled automatically if the direction stated that a failure to comply would lead to your appeal being struck out. Make sure that you always respond promptly.

- The tribunal does not have jurisdiction to deal with the appeal – eg, because there is no right of appeal against the decision.

- The tribunal considers that your appeal has no realistic prospect of success.

- You have failed to co-operate with the tribunal to the extent that the case cannot be dealt with 'fairly or justly'.

If your appeal is cancelled because you have not complied with a direction from the tribunal, you can apply for the appeal to be reinstated. You must do so in writing, and your application must be received within a month of the date of the letter telling you that your appeal has been struck out, although longer may be allowed. Your application should be accompanied by your reasons – eg, about why you could not reasonably comply with the direction.

In other situations, it is not possible to reinstate your appeal in this way. However, before your appeal is cancelled, you must first be given a chance to comment and say why the appeal should not be struck out – eg, why you had a good reason for not co-operating with the tribunal.

If your appeal has been struck out and/or the tribunal refuses to reinstate it, you can appeal further to the 'Upper Tribunal'.

2. How is your appeal decided?

There are two main ways in which your appeal can be decided:

- at a 'hearing'
- without a hearing, on the basis of the appeal papers

Under the normal rules, your appeal must be decided at a hearing, unless neither you nor the 'decision maker' (ie, at the DWP, HMRC or local authority) objects to the appeal being decided on the basis of the papers and the tribunal considers that a hearing is not necessary.

You are asked on the SSCS1 appeal form (or otherwise by 'HM Courts and Tribunals Service') if you want a hearing of your appeal. If you don't ask for a hearing at first but then decide that you do want one, you can still do so but should tell HM Courts and Tribunals Service as quickly as possible. It normally arranges for a hearing to take place, if you say that you want one. The hearing is an 'oral hearing' that you and, ideally, your 'representative' attend. The hearing can be by telephone or video call or in person (ie, with everyone in the room at a tribunal venue). You can request a hearing in any one of these ways, but HM Courts and Tribunals Service will decide how the hearing will take place. See also Box D.

> **What CPAG says**
>
> **Should you opt for a hearing?**
>
> It is strongly advisable to have your appeal decided at a hearing rather than on the basis of the papers. Hearings offer a chance for the tribunal to talk to you and find out more about your situation.
>
> Success rates at hearings are generally much higher than with appeals decided on the basis of the papers.
>
> However, if the tribunal contacts you to say that it can decide your appeal on the basis of the papers, it may indicate the decision it is minded to make. That would mean your appeal can be decided more quickly, and may be a strong indication of the likely outcome of your appeal even if you opt for a hearing, although it is not a guarantee. If the tribunal contacts you in this way, get advice from your representative (if you have one). For the things you should consider when your appeal can be decided more quickly, see page 118.

You and your representative, if you have one, are entitled to attend the hearing. The other 'parties to the appeal', such as the DWP or the local authority, can also attend the hearing.

Decided at a hearing

A hearing involves a discussion with the tribunal, whether it is conducted by telephone, by video call or in person at a tribunal venue. The tribunal asks you questions and finds out more about your situation – eg, about how your health condition affects you.

Attending the hearing is strongly advisable: you are much more likely to win your appeal. It is not essential that your representative attends the hearing with you, although if it is possible that is generally a good idea.

If there are very exceptional circumstances, a hearing can also take place in person at your home. This is called a **'domiciliary hearing'**.

6 / Deciding your appeal

This can be arranged if HM Courts and Tribunals Service accepts that you cannot get to a tribunal venue, and a telephone or video hearing is not possible. Domiciliary hearings are now rare.

Box D
Telephone, video call and in-person hearings

- There are no rules on whether the hearing should be by telephone, video call or in person. Which one to use is a matter of discretion for the judge. You can request a particular type of hearing, but the tribunal does not have to agree to it.

- The main rules and procedures on what happens are basically the same in all hearings. See section 3 of this chapter.

- If there is to be a telephone or video hearing of your appeal, HM Courts and Tribunals Service will send you information about the arrangements. HM Courts and Tribunals Service will want to be sure that such a hearing is practical – eg, that you can take part in a conversation with the tribunal.

- Generally, in-person hearings often offer the very best chance for you to communicate with the tribunal, as it can see and hear you very easily. For example, it can easily see your expression and your body language. But such a hearing requires attendance at a tribunal venue, and the tribunal may consider that the hearing can be dealt with adequately by telephone or video call.

- A telephone or video hearing may be more convenient for you – eg, because it avoids you having to travel. You may feel more comfortable being able to communicate from home.

- You may need to ensure that you are sufficiently private and comfortable at home to take part in a telephone or video hearing. Tell HM Courts and Tribunals Service about any problems you may have with taking part in the hearing.

- The need to speak clearly and allow other people in the hearing to speak may be even more important in a telephone or video hearing.

The tribunal clerk contacts you (or your representative) to arrange a date for the hearing and to inform you of where the hearing will be held. The clerk may allow you more time to gather evidence or get a representative, but does not have to. Be as clear as you can about why you need a later date and when that could be.

Decided on the papers

Deciding an appeal on the papers involves the tribunal looking at the papers but not holding a hearing. This can be a way of having your appeal decided more quickly. However, success rates are often much lower than they are for appeals which are decided at a hearing. If there is no further evidence to support your appeal, in many cases the tribunal will only have the evidence already collected and presented by the decision maker to consider.

It is not usually advisable to have your appeal decided on the papers. If you do want your appeal to be decided in this way, you can increase your chances of winning by preparing the appeal in the way described in Chapter 4.

In some cases, an appeal can be decided on the papers when the tribunal has already formed a view as to what the outcome of your appeal should be and it contacts you to say what decision it is minded to make. If you accept the decision the tribunal is minded to make, the decision is made on the papers. Success rates in these situations may be higher than in other cases in which the appeal is decided on the papers only.

How do you get ready for a hearing?

If you have a representative, you should discuss your case with them before the hearing. You should both be clear about what you consider to be the relevant facts, and what your case will be.

Be prepared for the tribunal to ask you questions about the relevant facts in your case. This is the most important part of the hearing. The questions will depend on what your appeal is about and the facts of your case. Being prepared for questioning does not mean that you should give prepared answers or behave in a particular way. You should respond to the tribunal's questions as honestly and as accurately as you can. Try neither to exaggerate nor to underestimate things when giving your answers, and be as clear as you can.

You will not be asked questions about the law, but your representative may be asked whether they have relied on a particular rule or piece of caselaw.

More information about how you are questioned, and the kind of questions you are asked, is on page 135.

What happens if you cannot attend the hearing?

If a hearing date has been set and this is not suitable, contact the tribunal clerk as soon as possible. Explain your situation and request a 'postponement' from the tribunal to an alternative date. Put your request in writing well in advance, although you can ask again on the day of the hearing if necessary. If you have said that you will attend a hearing but at the last minute find that you cannot or that you will be late, let the tribunal clerk know as soon as possible.

Remember that a tribunal is a court of law, and you are expected to attend if that is reasonable. When making your request, make sure you include your reasons why you cannot attend.

However, the tribunal does not have to agree to your request. It can proceed with the hearing in your absence in certain circumstances. This is when the tribunal is satisfied that you have been notified of the hearing and it is in the 'interests of justice' to proceed in your absence.

There is more about postponing or adjourning a hearing later in this section.

What happens if your representative cannot attend the hearing?

Your representative should do as much as they reasonably can to be available for a hearing if they wish to attend. Before it considers an alternative date, the tribunal expects your representative to have a good reason why they cannot attend and why there is no alternative representative available – eg, it may expect the advice centre to arrange for another representative to attend. If a particular date is not suitable, they should explain as soon as possible why this is the case, including, for example, why another representative cannot be there.

> Box E
> **Attending an appeal without your representative**
> - Make sure your representative has prepared a written 'submission' and sent this to the tribunal in advance. This is important, as it is the only statement by your representative of your case. It should state clearly that a representative will not be attending the hearing, but that you will.
> - The submission should point out any particular difficulties you are likely to encounter during the course of the hearing – eg, because of nervousness or embarrassment.
> - Ask your representative for a copy of the submission to take to the hearing.
> - You can be accompanied by someone, such as a friend or a relative, for general support and reassurance. Make it clear to the tribunal that this person is not acting as your representative.
> - Discuss your case with your representative before the hearing, so that you are prepared for the questions the tribunal may ask you.
> - Make an appointment with your representative for after the hearing to discuss what happened. Your representative can take notes in case they are useful if you appeal further to the 'Upper Tribunal'.

If your representative becomes unavailable at the last minute, you can request for the hearing to be 'postponed' – but the tribunal only has to do so if it considers that is fair and just.

In general, the appeal can proceed without your representative, especially if there is no explanation about why they cannot attend. However, the tribunal must still ensure that you get a fair hearing, and it should take your desire to be represented seriously. So if your representative is unavailable, the tribunal may postpone the hearing. If a postponement is needed on the day of the hearing, this is called an 'adjournment'. The tribunal does not have to do this: it depends on the facts of your case.

If your representative cannot attend a hearing (eg, because of limited resources in the advice centre), they can still do all the work involved in preparing your appeal, including sending a written submission to the tribunal on your behalf.

Even if your representative cannot attend the hearing, you should still attend so the tribunal can ask you questions.

Can the hearing be postponed?

Once a hearing date has been set, you can ask for it to be postponed (ie, put off) until a later date.

You must do this before the day of the hearing. A hearing can be postponed if the tribunal agrees that it needs to be put off so that the appeal can be dealt with properly – eg, because you cannot attend on the date that has been set, or your representative cannot attend and there is no one else that can attend in their place, and there is a good reason for not being able to attend.

Once a hearing has started, it can be 'adjourned' (paused). There is more about this on page 138.

There may be other reasons for requesting a postponement – eg, you expect to get important evidence but this may not arrive in time for the hearing. Contact the clerk of the tribunal to request that the tribunal grant a postponement. The tribunal does not have to agree to your request.

Whether or not a hearing is postponed depends on the facts of your case. The tribunal should bear in mind the need to deal with all cases 'fairly and justly', and should be prepared to consider your request. It must also deal with cases flexibly. The parties to the appeal are expected to co-operate with the running of the appeal, including making sure, as much as they can, that their case is ready. If a postponement is refused, you can still request an adjournment on the day of the hearing. If that is refused, the hearing takes place.

What the law says

Postponements and adjournments

The First-tier Tribunal may adjourn or postpone a hearing. If a party fails to attend a hearing, the tribunal may proceed in their absence if the tribunal is satisfied they have been notified of the hearing and considers that it is in the interests of justice to proceed.

Rules 5 and 31 The Tribunal Procedure (First-tier Tribunal) (Social Entitlement Chamber) Rules 2008

Checklist: before the hearing

Box F
Final preparations for the hearing

- Check that you or your representative have your appeal papers and a copy of your submission with you.

- Remember that the tribunal will ask you questions.

- Plan to be ready and comfortable in a suitable place (for a telephone or video hearing), or to arrive in good time at the tribunal venue (for an in-person hearing).

- You are not required to dress formally for a hearing. Ensure that you feel comfortable.

Box G
Checklist for representatives

- Check that both of you are familiar with the submission. It will damage your client's chances of winning their appeal if you say different things at the hearing.

- Ensure that your submission has been sent to the tribunal in advance, with any further evidence and any letters asking for such evidence. If you cannot do this at least seven days in advance of the hearing, tell the tribunal and send it in as soon as possible. Have electronic versions of the submission that can be shared (or additional paper copies if the hearing is in person). Remember that if you hand in your submission on the day, this may cause an adjournment.

- Think about the sort of questions the tribunal may ask your client and ensure they understand that you cannot usually answer for them.

- Make any witnesses aware of what the tribunal will be like and the sort of questions they may be asked.

- Have the appeal papers to hand, with key pages bookmarked or tabbed – these are likely to be referred to in the hearing. You may also wish to ensure you can access legislation that you think might be discussed. For example, you may wish to ensure that you have access to legislation.gov.uk or the relevant volume of the Sweet and Maxwell Social Security Legislation volumes. You may also find a guide such as CPAG's *Welfare Benefits Handbook* helpful for your own use, although the tribunal is not bound by such guides and usually will not want to consult them.

- Have writing materials to hand to make notes if you wish.

3. What happens at a hearing?

Tribunal 'hearings' take place on the date, and at the time and place, notified (unless there has been a 'postponement').

What the law says

Tribunal hearings

The tribunal may 'regulate its own procedure' and 'give a direction in relation to the conduct or disposal of proceedings at any time'.

Rule 5 The Tribunal Procedure (First-tier Tribunal) (Social Entitlement Chamber) Rules 2008

There are no set rules on exactly how a tribunal hearing must be run or the order in which things must happen. Instead, there are rules that give the tribunal wide discretion to decide what happens. The main requirement is that the hearing be fair – that everyone is given a chance to put their case, and that there is no bias.

The judge decides exactly what happens and in what order. This includes deciding, if necessary, that part of the hearing should be in private.

A typical hearing is as follows.

- The judge introduces the tribunal panel. The 'parties to the appeal' may be invited to outline their case.
- The tribunal asks questions. Most of the questions are to you – ie, the person who has made the appeal.
- The judge asks if there are any further questions or comments, after which the hearing ends and the tribunal considers its decision.

What happens when you arrive?

In a telephone or video hearing, you (and your 'representative', if you have one) are asked to be ready at least 20 minutes before the hearing is due to begin. In a telephone hearing, the clerk contacts you first. In a video hearing, you will have been sent an appropriate link and again first speak with the clerk. The clerk checks that you are ready to take part in the hearing. Then the call or video link is opened to the tribunal and the hearing begins.

In an in-person hearing, when you arrive at the tribunal venue, you wait in a waiting room. You are met by the tribunal clerk, who asks whether you have any expenses for attending the appeal, such as travel expenses or loss of earnings. You may also be able to submit claims for expenses – ask the clerk if this is possible. Your representative cannot claim expenses.

The clerk also asks whether you have any further evidence that you want to submit, and whether you have any witnesses. A witness could be someone like a friend or relative who can give evidence relevant to the appeal – such as how your health condition affects you.

If you do not have a representative, the clerk may give you a brief outline of what is likely to happen in the hearing. If you have any questions about this, ask them.

Depending on the venue, there may be other people in the waiting room. Usually, these are other claimants and their representatives, as the tribunal hears a number of cases each day. Someone from the DWP, HMRC or local authority (known as the 'presenting officer') may also be in the waiting room.

When the tribunal is ready to start, the clerk asks all the parties to the appeal (you, your representative and the presenting officer) into the tribunal room. If there is a witness, they are usually asked to wait outside the tribunal room until the tribunal is ready to ask them questions.

Who is the presenting officer?

Sometimes, there may be a representative from the body (eg, the DWP) that made the decision you are appealing. This person is called a presenting officer and is there to explain the decision.

A presenting officer represents a party to the appeal and so can make submissions and ask questions. Their role is supposed to be a 'friend of the court', to help the tribunal make its decision, not to defend the decision under appeal at all costs. The presenting officer may be in the waiting room or in a waiting room of their own. They should not be in the tribunal room until the hearing starts.

The presenting officer can ask you questions, although often they will not do so. They should not attempt to cross-examine you as if you were a witness or a defendant in a criminal trial – they should ask questions to help the tribunal make its decision.

What is the tribunal room like?

For in-person hearings, tribunal rooms differ slightly from venue to venue. In most cases, the tribunal members are seated on one side of a large table. They usually sit on normal chairs, not on a raised platform. The judge sits in the middle, with the other members of the tribunal (if present) alongside.

The parties to the appeal and their representatives are invited to sit on the other side of the table. You are usually asked to sit in the middle (opposite the judge), with your representative and the presenting officer to your side. The clerk sits on an adjoining side of the table, but often leaves and re-enters the room during the hearing. The clerk may be working at a computer during the hearing.

Who are the members of the tribunal?

Tribunals comprise one, two or three members, depending on the type of decision being appealed. There is always a judge with legal expertise. There is more information on this in Chapter 2.

The tribunal members do not wear judicial wigs or gowns. They are, however, likely to be dressed relatively formally, wearing suits or other smart clothes.

Who else may be present?

Usually, there is no one else present at the tribunal apart from the members of the tribunal, the parties to the appeal (you, your representative and, if present, the presenting officer) and the clerk.

Sometimes, someone undergoing training with 'HM Courts and Tribunals Service' may be present to observe the hearing. In an in-person hearing, they sit to the side or at the back of the room. You are asked if you are comfortable with them being present.

Witnesses may be present if they have been called by one of the parties to the appeal or under a 'direction' from the tribunal. In many appeals, there are no witnesses. If there are witnesses, the tribunal usually directs that they only take part in the hearing when it is their turn to be questioned.

In theory, in-person hearings are heard in public and any member of the public can attend. In practice, no one usually attends. If you want to protect your privacy, you can ask the tribunal to exclude members of the public. This issue should not arise in a telephone or video hearing.

How does the hearing begin?

First, the judge introduces the tribunal panel to you. Hearings are normally recorded. The judge explains this and asks everyone present (except the clerk) to introduce themselves for the recording.

The judge explains what the tribunal is and what its job is. They usually emphasise its independence.

Usually, the judge summarises what is at issue in the appeal and may invite the parties to outline their case, although they could move straight on to the evidence and questions.

This means that early in the proceedings the judge may ask your representative to outline the decision you are seeking, or whether there is anything to add to your written 'submission'.

The recording of the hearing is the 'record of proceedings'. This is not part of the decision but can be requested after the hearing.

Alternatively, the record of proceedings could be in the form of written notes made by the judge.

Can the tribunal decide your appeal straight away?

Sometimes, at the start of the hearing a tribunal may say that, having read the appeal papers, it can make a decision straight away – ie, without questioning you further at the hearing. This is not common, but can happen in some cases.

What the law says

Deciding the appeal straight away

There is nothing wrong in principle with a tribunal coming to a preliminary view on the basis of the appeal papers. Where a tribunal shares its preliminary view with the parties to the appeal, it should do so in a clear language which does not put pressure on the claimant to take any particular course. Language such as 'offer' is not appropriate. Where a tribunal shares its preliminary view and then changes its mind, it should consider whether the principles of natural justice and the overriding objective require it to alert the parties to that change before the close of proceedings. The reasons for the change of mind should be clearly recorded in the statement of reasons.

Upper Tribunal decision, KMN v Secretary of State for Work and Pensions (PIP) [2019] UKUT 42 (AAC)

If the decision does not give you all that you have asked for, you should not be pressured into accepting a decision straight away or be given the impression that you are being offered a deal. The tribunal should make it clear that if you decide to proceed with the hearing, the tribunal may change its mind, and the decision it makes may be more favourable or less favourable to you. If you have a representative with you, ask them for advice. Whether or not you have a representative, you should consider whether the tribunal is minded to give you everything that you have requested or, at least, that you have a reasonable chance of getting. Remember that at the hearing the tribunal will be also able to ask you questions and can change its mind about the decision it is minded to make.

If the hearing goes ahead and the tribunal changes its mind (and begins to think it will award you less than it suggested), the tribunal will often need to consider informing you before the hearing finishes. If the tribunal changes its mind, it should be made clear in the tribunal's 'statement of reasons' (there is more about the statement of reasons in Chapter 7).

How are you questioned?

The judge and the other members of the panel may all ask you questions.

The main aim of the questioning is to get oral evidence from you. This usually means that you are questioned about factual matters relevant to your appeal and the facts of your case. The tribunal will not ask you questions about the law. If you have a representative, they may ask them a question about the law, but if that happens this will often be to clarify or discuss something that they have said in their written submission.

For example, in a disability appeal you may be asked how far you can walk, whether you can concentrate on reading a magazine or watching a television programme, or about what happened at your medical examination. In an appeal about a 'sanction' applied to your universal credit for failure to attend a 'work-focused interview', you will be asked if you were notified about the interview and if so what your reasons for not attending were. In an appeal about an 'overpayment', you may be asked about what you told the benefits office about your circumstances, income and capital, and what happened afterwards. In appeals about the 'work capability assessment', personal independence payment and disability living allowance, one of the members of the tribunal is medically qualified and is likely to ask questions about your treatment and medication.

The tribunal usually tries to be friendly and should always be respectful, but can sometimes seem abrupt and business-like. The tribunal is not obliged to accept everything you say, and can decide not to believe you if it is contradictory or in conflict with other evidence which the tribunal places weight upon.

You may be asked some sensitive or embarrassing questions (eg, about your medical condition and how it affects your daily life), but this is often necessary to get the evidence required. The tribunal does not want your representative to answer for you. It may ask your representative some questions about your written submission, but often says relatively little to them. Your representative can indicate to the tribunal things like that they think you may have misunderstood a question, that something needs clarifying or that the questions are producing misleading answers in some way, although they may be asked by the judge to wait until the end.

If you become upset or confused by the questioning, indicate this to the judge and ask whether it is possible to slow down or rephrase the questions. Your representative can ask for this on your behalf. If you become very upset, the tribunal may allow a short 'adjournment'. In an exceptional case, the tribunal may allow your representative to speak for you.

At some point in the hearing, the tribunal usually asks the parties if they want to ask any questions. The judge decides when this happens. Your representative may want to ask you some questions to clarify a point that is important and has perhaps been misunderstood or ignored. The presenting officer may also ask questions.

The tribunal also questions any witnesses attending the hearing. For example, if a relative or carer has accompanied you to the hearing to give evidence about the sort of help you need at home, the tribunal asks them questions about this. Usually, the witnesses are not allowed to be present in the hearing until the tribunal is ready to ask them questions.

EXAMPLES

Questioning

Yasmin's representative thinks Yasmin has been confused by the questions the tribunal has asked, and asks the judge if she can put a question to Yasmin. The judge agrees, although he asks her representative to wait until the tribunal has finished asking questions.

Scarlett becomes upset during the hearing. Her representative indicates this to the judge and respectfully asks if the tribunal could put the questions in another way.

Tom's representative wants to give a lot of details about Tom's appeal at the start of the hearing. The judge asks the representative just to outline the basis of the appeal. The representative is given a chance to put his own questions to Tom, and make any other comments, before the hearing ends. When given the chance, the representative says the tribunal did not ask Tom about some important points in his submission, and asks the tribunal if it would like to ask Tom about them. The tribunal suggests that the representative asks Tom the questions.

Will the tribunal question a child, a vulnerable adult or sensitive witness?

Tribunals often decide not to question a child, even if they are the benefit claimant – eg, if they are getting disability living allowance. However, the tribunal should take account of the child's age, maturity and wish to take part in the proceedings and balance this with the need to take into account their welfare. Tell the tribunal in advance if you do not want your child to be at the hearing and be questioned – eg, because they are very young or too ill.

The tribunal will not question a vulnerable witness if their welfare would be harmed. Try to tell the tribunal in advance of any problems you may have with taking part in the hearing. If you (or someone who is a witness in your appeal) is vulnerable and you have a representative, your representative should alert the tribunal in advance and indicate any modifications the tribunal could make.

What the law says

Questioning children, vulnerable adults and sensitive witnesses

The tribunal only asks a child, vulnerable adult or sensitive witness questions if it considers it necessary for a fair hearing and that the person's welfare will not be 'prejudiced'. In deciding what to do, the tribunal should consider all the available evidence and, for example, what the child's parent or carer (or representative) says. The tribunal should take account of a child's age, maturity and wishes if they are participating in a hearing about their own appeal.

First-tier and Upper Tribunal Practice Direction, 'Child, Vulnerable Adult and Sensitive Witnesses', 30 October 2008; Upper Tribunal decision, JP v Secretary of State for Work and Pensions (DLA) [2014] UKUT 275 (AAC)

Can the hearing be adjourned?

Once a hearing has started, it can be 'adjourned' (paused) by the tribunal. This can be for a very short period before the hearing continues or until another day. An adjournment can be granted whenever the tribunal agrees there is a need to pause the hearing in order for the appeal to be dealt with properly. This could be, for example, to allow you and your representative to consider something that you have not been able to do before, or if the tribunal thinks it needs further evidence. You can ask the judge for an adjournment. The tribunal does not have to agree to your request.

Whether or not a hearing is adjourned depends on the facts of your case. The tribunal should bear in mind the need to avoid delay but deal with all cases 'fairly and justly', and should be prepared to consider your request. It must also deal with cases flexibly. The parties to the appeal are expected to co-operate with the running of the appeal, including making sure, as much as they can, that their case is ready.

In practice, a tribunal is often happy to grant a very short adjournment (such as for 10 minutes or so), but is reluctant to adjourn until another day. However, it may do so if you have new evidence or arguments on the day of the hearing, which it thinks the other party to the appeal must be given time to consider. A tribunal should also consider adjourning if it is considering making a less favourable decision in your case (such as by reducing your award), especially if you do not have a representative. If an adjournment is refused, the hearing goes ahead, and you and your representative must be prepared to continue.

What the law says

Adjourning an appeal

If an adjournment has been requested, the tribunal is likely to focus on the following questions. What would be the benefit of an adjournment? Why was the party not ready to proceed? What impact would an adjournment have on the other party and on the operation of the tribunal system?

Upper Tribunal decision, MHA v Secretary of State for Work and Pensions [2009] UKUT 211 (AAC)

Is there a medical examination?

The tribunal does not conduct a medical examination, except in industrial injuries disablement benefit cases. In an industrial injuries disablement benefit appeal, there is usually a pause in the proceedings and you are taken into an examination room to be examined by the medical member of the tribunal. In any other appeal, the tribunal is not permitted to examine you physically – so it cannot, for instance, ask you to remove an item of clothing.

However, the tribunal can observe your behaviour, such as your walking ability when you enter the tribunal room or your ability to remain comfortable throughout the hearing, and use those observations as evidence. So if, for example, you have taken extra pain-killing medication to enable you to take part in the hearing, explain that to the tribunal.

How does the hearing end?

When all the evidence has been heard by the tribunal, the judge usually asks whether there are any closing statements. This is your or your representative's chance to briefly sum up the case, highlighting strong points and emphasising any particular points that have come up during the hearing. If your representative wants to ask you any questions in order to clarify something or emphasise a point, the tribunal may allow them to do so.

At an in-person hearing, the parties to the appeal and their representatives are then asked to leave the tribunal room while the panel makes its decision. In a telephone or video hearing, the tribunal may leave the hearing to make its decision. Typically, this takes between 10 and 20 minutes.

In most cases, the tribunal makes its decision and gives it to you on the day, although it is not required to do so. If the judge thinks that a decision cannot be made on the same day and needs to be sent in writing later, they will say so.

When the tribunal has made its decision, at an in-person hearing usually you are invited back into the tribunal room to be informed. Sometimes, the tribunal may invite only your representative back, as tribunals often prefer to deal with the representative at this stage. However, if you wish to be present, this should normally be allowed. In a telephone or video hearing, usually the judge will tell you the decision. Sometimes, you are not informed of the decisoin until later, when you are sent the 'decision notice'.

The decision notice

The decision is usually given verbally by the judge, along with a short written decision notice, which contains the outcome of the appeal and a brief summary of reasons. This is the formal end to the hearing. It is not a further opportunity to make points or ask questions.

Sometimes, the tribunal posts the decision notice to you at a later date.

The decision notice should tell you that you can request a statement of reasons for the decision. The notes with the decision include the conditions for making a further appeal to the 'Upper Tribunal'. There is more information about this in Chapter 7.

If a presenting officer was at the hearing, they normally make sure that the organisation that made the original decision (eg, the DWP) gets the decision notice. If not, the clerk sends it.

4. What happens after the tribunal has made its decision?

Did you win your appeal?

If you win your appeal, usually the decision refusing you benefit is replaced with one awarding you benefit.

Although the tribunal decision is binding, the 'decision maker' is responsible for implementing it, not the tribunal. Sometimes, the decision maker may need to make further decisions about your entitlement – eg, if the tribunal has decided that you have a 'right to reside' for benefit purposes, the decision maker then needs to assess your income and capital. The tribunal has no legal power to enforce payment.

The decision maker can ask for a 'statement of reasons' for the tribunal's decision. This must normally be done within one month. This is done when the decision maker is considering whether to try to appeal to the 'Upper Tribunal'. There is more information on a statement of reasons in Chapter 7. If this is happening, payment of the benefit you were awarded in the appeal is suspended.

In the majority of cases, the decision maker does not appeal further. However, the decision maker may want to appeal to the Upper

Tribunal against the tribunal's decision when an important legal principle is at issue.

Can you be paid arrears?
If you win your appeal, you may be entitled to arrears of benefit that you were not entitled to until you won the appeal.

Sometimes, arrears are reduced. This can be to recover an outstanding 'overpayment' of benefit, or by the amount of another, 'overlapping' benefit that was paid to you while you were waiting for the appeal to be decided. An overlapping benefit is one that cannot be paid at the same time as another. For example, if you were paid jobseeker's allowance while waiting for your appeal about employment and support allowance to be decided, the two benefits will have overlapped and the arrears of your employment and support allowance are reduced by the amount of jobseeker's allowance you received. In general, arrears of personal independence payment and disability living allowance are not reduced.

Box H
Q&A: winning an appeal

Q: Kimberley's appeal was about the 'work capability assessment'. Does winning mean she will always have 'limited capability for work'?

A: No. The DWP can still arrange further medicals to assess her limited capability for work in the future. The tribunal may have recommended how long it should be before she is reassessed, but the DWP does not have to follow this. The same applies to decisions about the tests for personal independence payment and disability living allowance.

Q: Adam wins his appeal. When will he start getting his money?

A: There is no set period. In most cases, benefit starts to be paid again within a few weeks of the tribunal's decision. If there is a delay, contact the decision maker and ask for payment to begin as soon as possible.

Did you lose your appeal?

Box 1
Q&A: losing an appeal
Q: Laura was paid employment and support allowance while waiting for her appeal to be decided. Does she have to pay this back now that she has lost her appeal?

A: No. The decision maker only removes your entitlement from the date of the tribunal's decision, so Laura remains entitled to the employment and support allowance that she was paid – although her award now stops. She should get advice about what benefit she may be able to get instead of employment and support allowance.

Q: Rosalind lost her appeal about failing the work capability assessment for her universal credit claim. Can she try to get reassessed in the future?

A: Yes, but the request will be refused unless the decision about the assessment is now regarded as having been made in ignorance of a relevant fact, or based on a mistake about a relevant fact, or Rosalind has had a relevant change in her circumstances regarding her condition – eg, her health has deteriorated. She can still be entitled to universal credit even though she has failed the work capability assessment.

Q: Yuto lost his appeal about entitlement to personal independence payment. Can he reapply?

A: Yes, although any entitlement he may now have only starts from the date of his new claim. In practice, the decision maker may look to see whether there has been any change of circumstances that means they should not make the same decision as was made previously. But there is nothing to prevent a repeat claim.

If you lose your appeal, you have a number of options. Ask your 'representative' or an advice centre about what to do next.

- Consider whether the decision could be 'set aside' (this means it is cancelled and your appeal is heard again) or whether you can make a further appeal to the Upper Tribunal. There is more information about this in Chapter 7.

- If the tribunal awarded you some benefit, but not everything you asked for, and your circumstances have changed since the tribunal decision, consider asking the decision maker to look at the decision again and make a new decision on your entitlement. A decision that changes a decision made by the tribunal is called a 'supersession'. **Note:** even if the supersession increases your benefit award, you are only paid from the date you applied for the supersession.

- Accept the decision and if possible reclaim benefit (eg, if you now qualify because your circumstances have changed) or make a claim for a different benefit.

5. Deciding appeals about Scottish benefits

Appeals about the 'Scottish benefits' are dealt with by the 'Scottish Courts and Tribunals Service'. The 'First-tier Tribunal' that decides your appeal is very similar to the First-tier Tribunal that decides appeals about other benefits, so most of the information in this chapter applies.

There are a few differences. Once your appeal has been accepted as valid, the 'decision maker' at Social Security Scotland then has 31 days to produce a response to the appeal and send it to the tribunal. You are sent a copy of the response and are invited to reply or send in further evidence. There is a basic time limit of 31 days for doing this, starting with the date you receive the decision maker's response. You are treated as receiving the response two days after it was sent to you. In practice, you may be allowed to make comments in reply or send in other evidence after the basic time limit has passed, but you should explain why this has not been possible within the basic time limit – eg, because it took longer than that to get the evidence.

Like other tribunals, the tribunal is a court of law but is meant to be relatively informal, and has an overriding objective to deal with cases 'fairly and justly'. The most important differences for appeals about Scottish benefits are as follows.

- The legally qualified member of the tribunal is called the 'legal member', rather than the 'judge'.
- An instruction issued by the tribunal is called an 'order' rather than a 'direction'.
- The power of the tribunal to cancel an appeal is called the power to 'dismiss' the appeal, rather than 'strike out' the appeal.
- The tribunal may be composed differently and may consist of just a legal member.

Further information

General information about telephone and video appeals is available at gov.uk/guidance/what-to-expect-when-joining-a-telephone-or-video-hearing.

Chapter 7
After the appeal

This chapter covers:

1. Are you unhappy with the tribunal's decision?
2. Can the tribunal decision be changed?
3. Can you make a further appeal?
4. Appealing to the Upper Tribunal
5. After the appeal – Scottish benefits

What you need to know

- The tribunal's decision is usually given to you on the day of the 'hearing', but may be posted instead.
- You can request a 'statement of reasons' for the tribunal's decision. You should do this particularly if you lost your appeal and want to appeal further.
- A tribunal decision can be changed if there has been an accidental mistake or by being 'set aside' – ie, it is cancelled and reconsidered.
- You can make a further appeal to the 'Upper Tribunal' if there was an 'error of law' in the tribunal decision, but not simply because you disagree with it.

1. Are you unhappy with the tribunal's decision?

If you lost your appeal and you are unhappy with the decision, you may be able to get the decision changed or make a further appeal.

Getting the decision changed can be done relatively quickly, but there are very limited situations ('grounds') when this can be done. There is a right of further appeal to the 'Upper Tribunal' on a 'point of law'. In practice, this means that you have a right of further appeal if the tribunal's decision contains an 'error of law'. To show there is an error of law in the tribunal's decision, you usually need a 'statement of reasons' for the tribunal's decision.

> Box A
> **Scottish benefits**
>
> If the tribunal's decision is about one of the 'Scottish benefits', the rules and procedures for how you are notified of the decision and getting the decision changed are similar to those for decisions about other benefits, although there are some important differences. There is more about this in section 5 of this chapter.

How are you notified about the decision?

A short written statement of the tribunal's decision (the 'decision notice') is usually given to you on the day of the 'hearing'. Sometimes, the tribunal posts the decision notice to you at a later date.

The decision notice has accompanying notes which should tell you that you can request a statement of reasons for the decision, and include the conditions for making a further appeal to the Upper Tribunal.

The statement of reasons

It is important to have a statement of reasons if you want to appeal further to the Upper Tribunal. This is because there must be a point of law – usually, this means there must be an error of law in the decision in order to appeal to the Upper Tribunal. It is difficult to show that there is an error of law if there is no statement of reasons. You can request a statement of reasons from the tribunal.

> **What the law says**
>
> **Statements of reasons**
>
> A written statement of reasons must be supplied if a request is made within one month of the date on which the decision was given.
>
> Rules 33 and 34 The Tribunal Procedure (First-tier Tribunal) (Social Entitlement Chamber) Rules 2008

The statement of reasons is longer than the decision notice. It should include what the tribunal has decided are the facts of your case (known as the 'findings of fact') – eg, what the tribunal thinks are the relevant facts about your health condition and how this affects you. It should explain how it weighed the evidence – eg, what evidence the tribunal preferred (if any) and why it preferred it. Overall, you should be able to understand why the tribunal came to the decision that it did. Sometimes, the statement of reasons may be referred to as the 'full written decision' or 'written reasons'.

You must ask for a statement of reasons in writing. If your request is received by the tribunal within one month of the decision notice being given (or sent), it must provide one. If your request is outside the one-month time limit, the tribunal can still provide one, but does not have to. If your request is late, explain why.

The tribunal should send you a statement of reasons within a month of your request 'or as soon as is reasonably practicable' after that period.

The time limit for appealing to the Upper Tribunal does not start until the statement of reasons is sent. If there is a long delay, contact 'HM Courts and Tribunals Service' and ask what the reason for the delay is, and for the statement of reasons to be sent as soon as possible.

The record of proceedings

The 'record of proceedings' may consist of the recording of the hearing or, less commonly, the judge's written notes. It is not a formal part of the tribunal's decision. It is not usually sent to you as a matter of course, even if you request a statement of reasons.

If you want to appeal against a tribunal decision, it is not essential to have a record of proceedings. However, it is a good idea to request one at the same time as requesting a statement of reasons, as it can provide more background to the decision and help identify any errors of law.

You must apply for a record of the proceedings in writing within 18 months of the date of the tribunal's decision. The tribunal may still supply one if your request is made outside this time limit, but does not have to, and records of proceedings may be destroyed after six months. If you requested a record of the proceedings in time but the tribunal does not provide one, that is not automatically an error of law. But it may indicate that the decision itself is not as well founded as it should be, and so contains an error of law.

2. Can the tribunal decision be changed?

The tribunal decision can be changed if certain conditions are met. Unless it is changed, the decision is binding – ie, has to be applied.

What the law says

Clerical mistakes and set-asides

The tribunal may at any time correct any clerical mistake or other accidental slips or omissions in a decision.

The tribunal may set aside a decision which disposes of proceedings and remake the decision.

Rules 36 and 37 The Tribunal Procedure (First-tier Tribunal) (Social Entitlement Chamber) Rules 2008

If you want the tribunal decision to be changed, you should get advice from your 'representative' or an advice centre.

Any 'party to the appeal' can try to change a tribunal decision in one of the following ways.

- A clerical mistake or another accidental slip or omission can be corrected by the tribunal itself. This is to allow decisions to be altered quickly if there has been a simple error or 'slip of the pen'.
- In certain circumstances, the decision can be cancelled (called being 'set aside') and the appeal heard again.
- If there is a 'point of law' (usually this means an 'error of law') in the tribunal decision, it can be appealed further to the 'Upper Tribunal'. If you apply for a further appeal and there is a clear error of law, the First-tier Tribunal can review the decision before it is reconsidered by the Upper Tribunal. Usually, this leads to the appeal being heard again. **Note:** the 'decision maker' usually only tries to appeal further to the Upper Tribunal if the decision involves a general point of legal principle.
- If the decision includes an award of benefit, it can be looked at again by the decision maker if there are grounds to do so. This is called a 'supersession'. Usually, this happens if there has been a relevant change in your circumstances since the date of the decision – eg, if your medical condition changed while you were waiting for your appeal to be heard. A supersession cannot be carried out just because the decision maker thinks the decision is legally wrong. In this case, they must try to appeal to the Upper Tribunal.

When can the decision be cancelled?

A tribunal decision can only be cancelled (set aside) in certain circumstances. The main purpose is to allow a decision to be cancelled quickly if something went wrong with the tribunal procedure. Whether or not a decision can be set aside depends on the facts of your case.

The tribunal sets a decision aside if it considers that it is 'in the interests of justice' to do so and:

- a party to the appeal or their representative did not receive the appeal papers or other relevant documents in sufficient time for the 'hearing'
- a party to the appeal was not present at the hearing (except if they had chosen not to attend)
- there was some other 'procedural irregularity'

You must apply for a decision to be set aside in writing. This must be received by 'HM Courts and Tribunals Service' no later than one month after the date on which the tribunal decision was sent. In practice, as you are usually told the decision on the day of the hearing, this will be within one month of the date of the hearing. The tribunal can allow longer, but it does not have to. If your request is late, explain why.

When you ask for a decision to be set aside, you can also ask that if your request is refused, you be sent a 'statement of reasons' (because you may then want to consider whether there are grounds for a further appeal to the Upper Tribunal).

If the decision is set aside, the appeal must be heard again and a new decision made. If the decision is not set aside, the tribunal can treat your application as an application for permission to appeal to the Upper Tribunal or as an application to correct the decision.

If the tribunal refuses to set aside the decision, you may be able to appeal against this decision to the Upper Tribunal, as sometimes the reason for a set-aside may also be an error of law. For example, if relevant evidence was not included in the appeal papers, this is potentially both a ground for the decision to be set aside and an error of law because it breached the rules of 'natural justice'. If this applies to you, it may be worth trying to appeal to the Upper Tribunal about both the refusal to set aside and against the tribunal decision itself.

3. Can you make a further appeal?

Note: this guide only covers some very basic rules on further appeals. If you want to appeal further, you should speak to an experienced adviser.

If there is a 'point of law' (usually this means an 'error of law') in the 'First-tier Tribunal's' decision, you can appeal further to a different tribunal, called the 'Upper Tribunal'. All 'parties to the appeal' have the right of further appeal.

What the law says

Appealing to the Upper Tribunal

There is a right of appeal to the Upper Tribunal on any point of law arising from a decision made by the First-tier Tribunal, other than an excluded decision.

Section 11 Tribunals, Courts and Enforcement Act 2007

If you do not have a 'statement of reasons', it may be difficult to show that there has been an error of law.

You can appeal against most tribunal decisions, including a refusal to accept a late appeal. However, if the decision is not a final decision but is instead an 'interim' decision made before the appeal itself is decided (eg, a 'direction' made by the tribunal), you may be refused permission to appeal. In practice, in these cases it is usually better to ask the tribunal to change the decision.

There is a one-month time limit for applying for a further appeal, although this can be extended.

If the 'decision maker' intends to appeal further or is considering doing so and gives you written notice of this, payment of your benefit that was awarded after the tribunal decision can be suspended.

The Upper Tribunal is generally much less concerned with the particular facts and evidence in your case and much more concerned with whether the First-tier Tribunal applied the law properly.

7 / After the appeal

However, the Upper Tribunal has procedural rules that are similar to those that apply to the First-tier Tribunal. In particular, the 'overriding objective' is to deal with cases 'fairly and justly', which includes avoiding unnecessary formality. Parties should be able to participate fully in the proceedings, and have the right to appoint a 'representative', who need not be legally qualified.

> **Box B**
> **Appeals to the Upper Tribunal**
>
> - Appeals to the Upper Tribunal can only be on the basis of a point of law – usually this means an error of law.
> - Upper Tribunal appeals are more legalistic and can seem more formal than the First-tier Tribunal – eg, at a 'hearing' the decision maker is represented by a lawyer. However, unnecessary formality is supposed to be avoided.
> - All parties to the appeal have the right of further appeal to the Upper Tribunal.
> - You should have the statement of reasons for the tribunal's decision before trying to appeal to the Upper Tribunal.
> - You must apply for permission to appeal first. Your application must initially be made to the First-tier Tribunal, within the one-month time limit.
> - Decisions of the Upper Tribunal are binding on all decision makers and the First-tier Tribunal – they therefore affect all claimants, not just your individual case.

Do you need a representative?

You are not required to have a representative for an appeal to the Upper Tribunal. However, appeals to the Upper Tribunal are much more concerned with legal argument than most appeals to the First-tier Tribunal, and sometimes these can be complex. If you are not experienced in dealing with social security law, it is advisable to find a representative or, at least, get detailed advice. The decision maker is represented by a specialist in social security law or a lawyer.

Which decisions are excluded?

Some decisions cannot be appealed to the Upper Tribunal. These are mainly decisions the First-tier Tribunal makes about reviewing an earlier decision it made. In these cases, you can apply to the Upper Tribunal for a 'judicial review' of the decision.

What is an error of law?

There is no strict definition of an 'error of law' in a tribunal decision. It is a matter of judgement, taking into account the precise wording of the decision and the statement of reasons, and applying some general principles to that.

The fact that you disagree with the decision, or that someone else could have come to a different decision on the same facts, is not, in itself, an error of law.

The following are the most common errors of law in tribunal decisions.

- The tribunal gave inadequate reasons for its decision. The tribunal's reasons should enable you to see why it reached the decision it did. Sometimes, the reason for the decision may be obvious and the tribunal does not need to spell everything out. A decision is not wrong just because evidence produced later contradicts it. However, if the tribunal relied on a particular piece of evidence, or preferred one piece of evidence over another, it should say why.

- The tribunal made inadequate 'findings of fact' (ie, deciding the facts that were relevant to your appeal) for its decision, or the facts it found are such that it could not reasonably and correctly have made the decision that it did. The tribunal must establish sufficient facts to support its decision. If facts are disputed, the tribunal should say which version it prefers and why.

- The tribunal applied the law incorrectly – eg, it misinterpreted the wording in a particular part of the 'work capability assessment' or in the test for personal independence payment and so did not award you the correct points.

Other errors of law are possible, although are less common.

- The tribunal breached the rules of 'natural justice'. See Box C for what this means.
- The tribunal did not provide a statement of reasons for its decision when it had a duty to do so.
- The tribunal took things into account which it should not have, or refused to take into account things which it should have.
- The tribunal conducted a physical examination and based its decision on that (except in an industrial injuries disablement benefit case).

Box C
Natural justice

The principle of natural justice is a broad one, but essentially it means that each party to the appeal must be given a fair chance to put their case. The specific requirement for a tribunal to deal with a case 'fairly and justly' is part of this.

Showing that a tribunal has breached the rules on natural justice can be difficult, as much depends on the facts of your case – getting the 'record of proceedings' may help. Examples can include if the tribunal held the hearing in your absence even though you intended to be there, or did not give you an adequate warning that it was minded to make a less favourable decision than the one you appealed against. The fact that you found the tribunal abrupt or unfriendly is not enough.

4. Appealing to the Upper Tribunal

How do you apply for permission to appeal?

You must apply in writing to the 'First-tier Tribunal' for permission to appeal to the 'Upper Tribunal', with details of your 'grounds' of appeal (ie, the error(s) of law that you think are in the decision) and the decision that you want made instead. If you are refused, you can apply directly to the Upper Tribunal.

The 'decision maker' can also apply for permission to appeal. If the decision maker applies for permission to appeal within the time limit, payment of any benefit awarded to you as a result of the tribunal decision can be suspended.

The judge who considers your application for permission to appeal to the Upper Tribunal may not be the same judge who was on the tribunal that heard your appeal.

What decisions can the First-tier tribunal make?

The judge can do any of the following.

- Review the First-tier Tribunal decision (so that the appeal is heard again), if they are satisfied that there is an 'error of law' in it. This only applies in very clear cases but is common.

- Grant you permission to appeal. You are notified of this, and you must then send a 'notice of appeal' to the Upper Tribunal so that it is received within one month of your being sent the permission to appeal. You are sent Form UT1 on which to do this. The Upper Tribunal can extend the time limit but does not have to. If you send the notice of appeal late, explain why. You should include the notice granting you permission to appeal and a copy of the tribunal's decision and 'statement of reasons' (if you have one).

- Refuse you permission to appeal. You must be notified of this in writing, including reasons for the refusal and notice of your right to apply directly to the Upper Tribunal for permission to appeal.

If there is no statement of reasons for the tribunal's decision because no one has applied for one, the judge must first treat your application as an application for a statement of reasons. If a statement of reasons is then provided, you must apply for permission to appeal again. If a statement of reasons is refused (eg, because you apply outside the time limit), the judge can either refuse or grant you permission to appeal.

Has the judge reviewed the decision?
If the judge reviews the decision, you must be notified of the outcome and of any further right of appeal you may have. The judge can:

- correct accidental errors in the decision
- amend the reasons given for the decision (but not add new reasons the tribunal had not previously considered)
- cancel the decision. The tribunal must then either make a new decision or (in practice, less commonly) refer it to the Upper Tribunal

Generally, you cannot appeal against a decision to review (or not to review) the decision of the tribunal. However, you can appeal against any new final decision on your appeal.

If the decision is reviewed and a new decision made by the First-tier Tribunal, you have the same right of appeal against the new decision as you had with the original decision. You can apply for a statement of reasons and ask for permission to appeal.

Has the First-tier Tribunal refused you permission to appeal?
If the judge refuses to give you permission to appeal to the Upper Tribunal, you can reapply directly to the Upper Tribunal. Your application should be received by the Upper Tribunal no later than one month after the date the First-tier Tribunal's refusal was sent. The Upper Tribunal can allow a longer period, but does not have to. If your application is late, explain why.

Your application to the Upper Tribunal must be in writing. Ideally, it should be on Form UT1, available from 'HM Courts and Tribunals Service', as using that should ensure your application is made in the correct way. If you have a 'representative' who is legally qualified (or is supervised by such a person), they must send your appeal form and any documents associated with it using the official CE-File service (via gov.uk).

Your application must include your details and those of your representative and identify the First-tier Tribunal decision you are appealing. It must also include:

- the alleged error of law in the decision
- copies of the decision, the statement of reasons (if you have one) and the notice of the First-tier Tribunal's refusal to grant you permission to appeal
- the reasons why you are late in applying for permission to appeal, if applicable

However, the Upper Tribunal can ignore any irregularities in your application. If you do not have a statement of reasons, the Upper Tribunal can still grant you permission to appeal. You must still show that there is an error of law in the tribunal's decision – and this is more difficult without a statement of reasons. If the tribunal does not provide a statement of reasons when it has a duty to do so (ie, if you requested one within the one-month time limit), this, in itself, is an error of law.

What can the Upper Tribunal do?

The Upper Tribunal decides whether or not to grant you permission to appeal and sends you written notice of this.

If you are given permission, the Upper Tribunal gives instructions on how your appeal goes ahead.

It can decide there was no error of law so that the decision of the First-tier Tribunal stands or allow the appeal because the decision contains an error of law. In this case, the Upper Tribunal either decides itself what the correct decision should have been or sets aside (cancels) the First-tier Tribunal's decision and orders a new tribunal to reconsider the appeal.

The Upper Tribunal may hold a 'hearing' of your application for permission to appeal or the appeal itself. In most cases, hearings are not held.

If you are refused permission by the Upper Tribunal, this means your appeal does not go ahead. You cannot appeal any further.

Judicial review in the Upper Tribunal

In a few cases, there is no right of appeal to the Upper Tribunal against a decision of the First-tier Tribunal. These are cases in which the tribunal has made an 'excluded decision', such as a decision to review its own earlier decision. It may be possible to apply for a 'judicial review' of the excluded decision and have that considered by the Upper Tribunal, although this is rare. Judicial reviews can involve legal costs, so get advice from a solicitor about what you may have to pay. In Scotland, you must apply first to the Court of Session, which may then transfer your application to the Upper Tribunal.

Appealing to the higher courts

Decisions of the Upper Tribunal can sometimes be the subject of further appeals. These appeals are to the higher courts – the Court of Appeal in England and Wales and the Court of Session in Scotland. Such appeals can only be on the basis of a 'point of law' (usually this means an error of law) in the Upper Tribunal's decision and are wholly concerned with legal argument. After that, still further appeals are possible, again on the basis of an error of law, to the Supreme Court. Appeals to the higher courts can involve legal costs and you should consider obtaining legal advice from a solicitor. Before making any application, get advice about what you may have to pay.

5. After the appeal – Scottish benefits

If your appeal is about one of the 'Scottish benefits', how you are notified of the decision is the same as for other benefits. However, unlike for other benefits, the tribunal can publish its decisions. Your anonymity must be protected and you can ask that the published version be edited – eg, to protect your privacy.

As for other benefits, you can request a 'statement of reasons' for the tribunal's decision, but for Scottish benefits the time limit is 31 days of

7 / After the appeal

being notified, rather than a month. However, it is understood that in most cases a statement of reasons will be produced and sent out to you automatically.

If you are unhappy with the tribunal's decision, you can challenge it. As for other benefits, this has to be on the basis of an 'error of law', not simply because you disagree with it. There are two ways to challenge the decision:

- request a 'review' by the 'First-tier Tribunal'
- make a further appeal to the 'Upper Tribunal'

As for other benefits, the First-tier Tribunal can correct a clerical mistake, or an accidental slip or omission. Unlike for other benefits, there is no power for the tribunal to 'set aside' its decision.

What CPAG says

Should you request a review or appeal to the Upper Tribunal?

If you are unhappy with the decision of the First-tier Tribunal about a Scottish benefit, you can choose how to challenge it. Bear in mind the following, and get advice if you are unsure.

- A request for a review is automatically also treated as being an application for permission to appeal to the Upper Tribunal.
- You can just apply for permission to appeal to the Upper Tribunal instead of asking for a review, but a review provides an extra opportunity to argue that the tribunal's decision contains an error of law.
- The time limit for requesting a review is quite short (14 days).
- If you apply for a review, there may be a 'hearing' which will normally be held before the same legal member who was on the tribunal of your appeal.
- If the tribunal decision contains an obvious error of law, a review may be a quicker way of getting the decision changed.
- If you appeal to the Upper Tribunal, its decision may affect future cases which are similar to yours, while a review does not.

A request for a review must be made in writing and received by the First-tier Tribunal within 14 days of the date of the decision or, if later, the date the statement of reasons was sent to you. Your request must identify what error of law the tribunal has made. Your request is also treated as a request for permission to appeal to the Upper Tribunal – unless you expressly request that it is not. When the tribunal notifies you of its decision, you are asked if you wish to proceed with an appeal to the Upper Tribunal.

Appeals to the Upper Tribunal for Scottish benefits are very similar to appeals to the Upper Tribunal for other benefits. However, the basic time limit for requesting permission to appeal is that your request must be received within 30 days, rather than one month.

If you are granted permission to appeal, or if the First-tier Tribunal has refused you permission to appeal, to make your appeal/apply direct for permission to appeal, use Form UTS-1 available from the 'Scottish Courts and Tribunals Service'.

Further information

There is more information about appeals to the Upper Tribunal and the courts in CPAG's *Welfare Benefits Handbook*.

CPAG's Upper Tribunal assistance project can provide help to advisers in England and Wales helping claimants challenge tribunal decisions. See cpag.org.uk/upper-tribunal-assistance-project. CPAG also provides training and advice to support advisers to pursue judicial review remedies. See cpag.org.uk/jrproject.

Appendix

Glossary of terms

Adjourned/adjournment
A pause in an appeal hearing – eg, to allow one party to the appeal to consider a new point or to get more evidence.

Allow
The tribunal agrees, at least in part, that the decision being appealed is wrong.

Appointee
Someone, usually a relative, who is authorised by the DWP or HMRC (or, for the Scottish benefits, by Social Security Scotland) to claim benefits on another person's behalf if they cannot claim for themself.

Care component
The part of disability living allowance or child disability payment paid for a person with care needs.

Claimant
The person who has claimed benefit and made an appeal.

Clearance time
The time it takes for an appeal to be heard and decided by the appeal tribunal.

Couple
Two people living together who are married or civil partners, or who are living together as if they were married or civil partners.

Daily living component
The part of personal independence payment or adult disability payment paid if you have problems with daily living activities, or are terminally ill.

Decision maker
An officer in the DWP (or for Scottish benefits, Social Security Scotland), HMRC or local authority who makes the original decision, and who considers a request for the decision to be looked at again.

Decision notice
A short written summary of the tribunal's decision. Also, the letter from the decision maker, informing you of the decision about your benefit claim.

Descriptor
A statement used for personal independence payment or adult disability payment, describing your ability to carry out one of the specific daily living or mobility activities.

Determination
In Scotland, the name given to a decision on entitlement to a Scottish benefit.

Direction (or for an appeal about a Scottish benefit, an order)
An instruction from the tribunal requiring something to be done.

Domiciliary hearing
An in-person hearing of an appeal taking place in the claimant's home, rather than at a tribunal venue. Now rare in practice.

Error of law
A legal mistake in the tribunal's decision.

Expediting
The process by which the tribunal clerk speeds up the arrangement of an appeal hearing so that it is heard earlier than it might otherwise have been.

Findings of fact
The facts established and recorded by a tribunal that are relevant to the appeal.

First-tier Tribunal (for Scottish benefits, First-tier Tribunal for Scotland)
The independent tribunal that considers appeals against benefit and tax credit decisions made by the DWP (for Scottish benefits, Social Security Scotland), HMRC and local authorities.

Grounds
The reasons for the appeal.

Hearing
The way in which tribunals decide appeals involving oral evidence from claimants. Conducted by telephone or video call, or in-person at a tribunal venue.

HM Courts and Tribunals Service
The body that administers and conducts the independent hearing of an appeal (except for Scottish benefits).

Judicial review
A way of challenging in court the decisions of government departments, local authorities and some tribunals against which there is no right of appeal.

Lapse
The process of replacing a decision being appealed before the appeal is heard.

Limited capability for work
A test of whether a person's ability to work is limited by a health condition.

Limited capability for work-related activity
A test of how severe a person's health problems are and whether their ability to prepare for work is limited.

Mandatory reconsideration
The requirement to have a decision looked at again, via a revision (for benefits), by the decision maker before an appeal can be made.

Mandatory reconsideration notice
The letter in which the outcome of a mandatory reconsideration is sent to the claimant.

Means-tested benefit
A benefit that is only paid if someone's income and capital are low enough.

Mobility component
The part of personal independence payment or adult disability payment paid if you have mobility problems (or for a child with

mobility problems in disability living allowance or child disability payment).

Natural justice
The concept that includes allowing each party to the appeal to be given a fair chance to put their case.

Official error
An error by, for example, someone at the DWP, HMRC or a local authority which results in a benefit decision being wrong.

Overpayment
An amount of benefit that is paid which is more than a person's entitlement.

Parties to the appeal
The person who has made the appeal and the body that made the decision being appealed.

Presenting officer
A representative from the body that made the decision being appealed who attends an oral hearing to assist the tribunal.

Postponed/postponement
Putting off a tribunal hearing, before it has started, so that it begins on a later date.

Record of proceedings
The electronic recording of the appeal hearing, or notes made of a tribunal hearing by the judge, recording the submission, evidence and procedural matters such as any consideration of adjournment.

Redetermination
In Scotland, the name given to the statutory process that allows a determination about entitlement to a Scottish benefit to be changed.

Representative
Someone who helps a claimant to put their case to the tribunal.

Review
For Scottish benefits, the process in the law that allows a First-tier Tribunal to change its decision on the basis of an error of law.

Revision
A process in the law that allows benefit decisions to be changed.

Right to reside
A social security test, mainly affecting European Economic Area nationals, which must be satisfied in order to claim certain benefits.

Sanction
A reduction in a person's benefit award for failing to meet certain work-related requirements.

Scottish benefits
Benefits introduced in Scotland under social security powers devolved to the Scottish government.

Scottish Courts and Tribunals Service
The body that administers and conducts the independent hearing of an appeal about Scottish benefits.

Secretary of State for Work and Pensions
The government minister with overall responsibility for the DWP. Formally speaking, the person who makes decisions on benefits administered by the department.

Set aside
Cancelling a tribunal decision on certain grounds.

Slips of the pen
Minor accidental errors in a tribunal's written decision, which can be corrected by the tribunal.

Social Entitlement Chamber
The part of HM Courts and Tribunals Service that deals with appeals about benefits.

Social Security Chamber
The part of the Scottish Courts and Tribunals Service that deals with appeals about Scottish benefits.

Statement of reasons
A written statement from the tribunal explaining why it came to its decision.

Struck out (or, in an appeal about a Scottish benefit, dismissed)
When an appeal is cancelled before it has been considered.

Submission
An argument or setting out a case, usually in writing, which is put to the tribunal.

Supersession
A process in the law allowing benefit decisions to be changed, usually as a result of a change in circumstances.

Tribunal clerk
The official responsible for administering an appeal, including arranging the hearing and providing administrative support to the tribunal.

Uphold
Allow an appeal – ie, agree, at least in part, that the decision is wrong.

Upper Tribunal (for Scottish benefits, the Upper Tribunal for Scotland)
The independent judicial body that considers further appeals against decisions of First-tier Tribunals.

Waive
When the tribunal uses its legal discretion so that it does not insist that a procedural rule be observed.

Weighing evidence
The process by which a tribunal decides how much it should be influenced by a particular piece of evidence in coming to its decision.

Work capability assessment
A social security test used to decide whether someone is too ill to work in universal credit and employment and support allowance.

Work-focused interview
A compulsory interview with the DWP to discuss job opportunities, barriers to work and training.

Index

A
adult disability payment
    evidence of disability 112
allowing an appeal 18
appeal forms 44
    where to send forms 47
appeal hearing 122, 130
    adjournments 138
    after the hearing 141
    attendance of representative 125
    attending the hearing 17, 125
    children 137
    closing statements 140
    decision 140
    decision at start of hearing 134
    domiciliary hearings 18, 122
    in person, by telephone or video call 121
    introductory proceedings 133
    members of the tribunal 132
    postponements 127
    preparing for the hearing 124
    questioning 135
    record of proceedings 149
    representatives 4
    vulnerable adults 137
    where does hearing take place 16
appeal tribunals 11, 57
    fair and just process 57
    First-tier Tribunal 11
    inquisitorial role 57
    representatives 58
    Scottish Courts and Tribunals Service 22
    Upper Tribunal 152
appeals 1
    after an appeal 146
    after appeal is made 115
    appeals system 10
    avoiding an appeal 8
    cancelling an appeal 120
    deciding an appeal 114
    deciding whether to appeal 6
    decisions made on appeal papers 124
    delays 116
    getting a decision quickly 118
    grounds for appeal 46
    hearings 121, 122
    how appeal is decided 121
    how long does an appeal take 21
    invalid appeals 48
    lapsed appeal 116
    losing an appeal 143
    making an appeal 25
    more than one appeal 15, 104
    online appeals 44
    preparing an appeal 56
    Scottish benefits 22, 48, 144
    time limits 40
    valid appeals 43
    what is an appeal 2
    who can appeal 27
    winning an appeal 141
    withdrawing an appeal 119
appointees 27
arrears of benefits 142

B
balance of probability 57
benefit decisions
    appeal forms 44
    appeal process 2, 26, 115
    decision notice 26
    decisions that can be appealed 3, 28
    mandatory reconsideration notice 33
    mandatory reconsiderations 31
    time limit for appeals 40

C
cancellation of appeal 120
caselaw 66
change of circumstances
    evidence 77
    medical conditions 103
    supersessions 35
changing a decision 19, 149
child disability payment
    evidence of disability 112
clearance times 22
clerical errors 150
compensation 21
complaints
    administration 21
costs 21
Court of Appeal 159
Court of Session 159

D
decision maker 2
    mandatory reconsiderations 32
    response to appeal 115
decision notice 26, 140, 147
decisions
    benefit decisions 2, 26
    process decisions in Scotland 53
    Scottish benefits 49

Index

tribunal decisions 140
determinations 49
disability appeals 4, 92
   condition changes 103
   disability qualified tribunal member 13
   domiciliary hearings 18, 122
   evidence from another benefit claim or appeal 104
   evidence of disability 112
   less favourable decision 106
   medical evidence 94
   winning an appeal 109
disability living allowance
   evidence of disability 112
disability qualified tribunal member 13
domiciliary hearings 18, 122

E
error of law 152
   definition 154
evidence
   change of circumstances 77
   examples 74
   further evidence 75
   medical evidence 94
   preparing for an appeal 71
   relevant evidence 73
   weighing evidence 76
expenses 131

F
First-tier Tribunal 11
   composition of tribunal 13
   membership 12, 132
   more than one appeal 15
   permission for further appeal 156
   powers of tribunal 18
   reviewing a decision 156
   tribunal venue 16
forms
   appeal forms 44
further appeal 152
   appeal to Upper Tribunal 156

G
grounds for appeal 46

H
HM Courts and Tribunals Service 11

I
illness appeals 4, 92
   condition changes 103
   evidence from another benefit claim or appeal 104
   less favourable decision 106
   medical evidence 94
   winning an appeal 109
information
   included in appeal 45

J
judge 12
judicial review 159

L
late appeals 41
legislation 66
less favourable decision 20
limited capability for work 93
losing an appeal 143

M
mandatory reconsiderations 31
   applying for reconsideration of benefit decision 35
   late requests 37, 38
   mandatory reconsideration notice 40
   time limit for reconsideration of benefits 33, 35
medical evidence 94
   charges for evidence 97
   evidence from another benefit claim or appeal 104
   refusal by doctor to supply evidence 95
   relevant evidence from doctor 98
   weighing evidence 101
medical examination 139
medical practitioner 13
mistakes
   clerical errors 150
   errors of law 152
   official error 39

N
natural justice 155

O
official error 39
online appeals 44
oral hearing 121
overpayments 30

P
personal independence payment
   evidence of disability 112
   new decision before appeal heard 117

Index

preparing an appeal 61
  checking the law 65
  complex legal issues 70
  facts and evidence 71
  relevant facts 72
  relevant law 67
  submissions 78
  what is the point of the appeal 62
presenting officer 131

R
reconsiderations
  mandatory reconsiderations 31
record of proceedings 149
redeterminations 50
  late request 51
  requesting a redetermination 50
  time limits 51
representatives 4, 58
  attendance at hearings 125
  attending without a representative 126
  checklist for hearing 129
  finding a representative 5
  role 59
  Upper Tribunal 153
revisions 33

S
Scottish benefit appeals 22
  after an appeal 159
  deciding an appeal 144
  late request for appeal 52, 54
  making an appeal 48
  process decision appeals 53
  redeterminations 50
  time limits for appeals 52, 54, 144
  valid appeals 52
Scottish benefits 23
  determinations 49
  process decisions 53
  redeterminations 50
Scottish Courts and Tribunals Service 24
Social Entitlement Chamber 11
social security law 66
  relevant law 67
statement of reasons 147
striking out 120
submissions 78
  basic principles 79
  sample written submissions 81

substantial risk rule 110
supersessions 35, 150

T
time limits
  appeals 40
  mandatory reconsideration of benefits 33, 35
  missing a mandatory reconsideration time limit 37, 38
  missing an appeal time limit 41
  redeterminations 51
  Scottish benefit appeals 52, 54
travel expenses 131
tribunal clerk 12
tribunal decisions 140, 146
  cancelling a decision 150
  changing a decision 19, 149
  excluded decisions 154
  less favourable decisions 20
  making a decision quickly 118
  notification of a decision 147
  set aside 150
  statement of reasons 147

U
upholding a decision 18
Upper Tribunal
  appealing a First-tier Tribunal decision 152, 156
  decisions as caselaw 66
  excluded decisions 154
  further appeals 152
  judicial review 159
  permission to appeal 158
  refusal of permission to appeal 157

V
valid appeals 43
  appeal not valid 48
  Scottish benefits 52

W
winning an appeal 6, 141
  benefit arrears 142
withdrawing an appeal 119
witnesses 131, 133
work capability assessment rule 93
  appeals 110
  substantial risk rule 110